The Complete Handbook of Science Fair Projects

NEWLY REVISED AND UPDATED

Julianne Blair Bochinski

Illustrated by Judy DiBiase

WILEY

John Wiley & Sons, Inc.

To my nephews Andrew and Alexander.

Published by John Wiley & Sons, Inc., Hoboken, New Jersey
Published simultaneously in Canada.

Design and production by Navta Associates, Inc.

The publisher and the author have made every reasonable effort to ensure that the experiments and activities in the book are safe when conducted as instructed but assume no responsibility for any damage caused or sustained while performing the experiments or activities in this book. Parents, guardians, and/or teachers should supervise young readers who undertake the experiments and activities in this book.

For general information about our other products and services, please contact our Customer Care Department within the United States at (800) 762-2974, outside the United States at (317) 572-3993 or fax (317) 572-4002.

Wiley also publishes its books in a variety of electronic formats. Some content that appears in print may not be available in electronic books. For more information about Wiley products, visit our web site at www.wiley.com.

ISBN 0-471-45767-1 (cloth : alk. paper)
ISBN 0-471-46043-5 (paper : alk. paper)

Printed in the United States of America

10 9 8 7 6 5 4 3 2 1

CONTENTS

Foreword to the Newly Revised Edition   vii

Acknowledgments   ix

SI (Metric) Conversion Table   xii

Introduction   1

PART I   A Complete Guide to Science Fair Projects   3

Chapter 1   Science Fairs and Science Fair Projects   5
Chapter 2   Before You Get Started   9
Chapter 3   Getting Started   13
Chapter 4   Planning and Conducting Your Experiment   26
Chapter 5   Organizing and Presenting Data   35
Chapter 6   The Display: Putting It All Together for the Fair   42
Chapter 7   At the Fair   50

PART II   50 Award-Winning Science Fair Projects   57

1. Which Characteristic Is Most Influential in Attracting Bees to a Flower: Fragrance, Color, or Flavor? (Behavioral Science)   59

2. The Effects of Gender Identity on Short-Term Memory (Behavioral Science)   62

3. Do All Plants Transpire at the Same Rate under Different Sources of Light? (Botany)   65

4. Can Plant Cloning Be Used Effectively by Produce Growers? (Botany)   68

5. How Effective Is Beta Carotene in Fighting Cancer in Plants? (Botany)   70

6. The Effect of Electromagnetic Fields on *Eremosphaera* Algae Cells (Botany)   73

7. What Is the Most Efficient Substance for Melting Ice? (Chemistry)   76

8. What pH Level Is Most Conducive to Corrosion in Iron and Copper? (Chemistry)   78

9. How Effective Is Lobster Shell Chitin in Filtering Wastewater Metallic Ions? (Chemistry)   80

10. How Does Saltwater Mix in an Estuary? (Chemistry)   83

11. Can the Life Span of a Soap Bubble Be Extended in Different Temperatures and Atmospheric Conditions? (Chemistry)   86

12. What Colored Dyes Are Found in Powdered Drink Mix and Colored Marking Pens? (Chemistry)   89

13. Can Mathematical Patterns Be Found in Johann Sebastian Bach's Two-Movement Preludes and Fugues? (Computer Science/Mathematics)   92

14. Measuring the Brightness of an Incandescent Light Bulb (Energy)   94

15. Which Form of Insulation Is Most Effective? (Energy)   97

16. Alcohol as a Fuel: Recycling Wastes into Energy (Energy)   99

17. Can Earthworms Be Used to Recycle Kitchen Wastes into Fertile Garden Soil? (Environmental Science)   102

18. The Great American Lawn and Pristine Water: Can They Coexist? (Environmental Science)   105

19. Do Gas Stations Affect the Soil Around Them? (Environmental Science)   107

20. What Is the Effect of #6 Heating Oil on *Elodea densa* in an Aquatic Environment? (Environmental Science)   110

21. Can Limestone Be Used to Protect Pine Trees from Acid Rain? (Environmental Science)   112

22. What Section of a Town Has the Most Pollution in the Form of Airborne Particles? (Environmental Science)   114

23. Environmental Effects on the Biodegradability of Plastic Bags, Paper Bags, and Newspaper (Environmental Science)   116

24. How Does Acid Rain Affect the Cell Structure of *Spirogyra?* (Environmental Science)   118

25. The Presence of Heavy Metals in a Coastal Body of Water and Their Effect on Aquatic Life (Environmental Science)   121

26. What Substance Is Most Effective for Cleaning Teeth? (Health Science)   125

27. The Relationship between Alcohol Dosage and Dependency in a Rat (Health Science)   127

28. How Effective Are Various Items in Protecting against Ultraviolet Radiation? (Health Science)   130

29. The Wave, the Golden Mean, and $r = \left[\dfrac{2}{\left(-1 + \sqrt{5}\right)} \right]^{\wedge} \theta$ (Mathematics)   133

30. Are Dandelions as Effective as Commonly Prescribed Antibiotics against Bacteria? (Microbiology)   138

31. Can Food Molds Be Used to Reduce Bacteria Spread by a Pet Rabbit? (Microbiology)   141

32. What Substance Is Most Effective for Preventing the Breeding of Bacteria in Waterbeds? (Microbiology)   143

33. How Can the Amount of Bacteria Found on Kitchen Sponges and Dishcloths Be Reduced? (Microbiology)   146

34. An Analysis of the Bacteria and Heavy Metal Content of Sewage before and after Treatment at a Sewage Plant (Microbiology)   148

35. Are Your Clams Safe to Eat? (Microbiology)   150

36. Footwear versus Bacteria (Microbiology)   152

37. The P-Trap: A Bacteria Cauldron (Microbiology)   154

38. The P-Trap: A Continuing Dilemma (Microbiology)   157

39. Improving the Antibacterial Effects of Garlic (Microbiology)   160

40. Does the Period of Motion of a Pendulum Depend on Its Weight, Amplitude, or Length? (Physics)   164

41. Are Composites of Wood Stronger than Solid Wood? (Physics)   167

42. Which Angle of Attack Generates the Most Lift? (Physics)   170

43. Polarization and Stress Analysis of Airplane Windows (Physics)   172

44. Shape and Viscous Effect (Physics)   175

45. What Would Happen to Climate, Weather Patterns, and Life Forms if the Earth Were Cubical? (Physics)   178

46. The Physics of Cheating in Baseball (Physics)   181

47. Does a Golf Ball's Bounciness Influence the Distance that It Will Travel? (Physics)   185

48. Relaxing the Breathing Patterns of Newly Purchased Pet Fish so They May Adapt to a New Aquarium (Zoology)   188

49. Can the Heartbeat of a Chicken Embryo Be Detected without Breaking Its Eggshell? (Zoology)   190

50. Are Dogs Colorblind? (Zoology)   193

PART III   Appendixes

Appendix A   400+ Ideas for Science Fair Project Topics   195

Appendix B   100+ Project Titles of Award-Winning Projects   205

Appendix C   Scientific Supply Companies   209

Appendix D   State, Regional, and International Science and Engineering Fairs   211

Appendix E   Alternative Science Fair Project Competitions   221

Glossary   224

Index   227

FOREWORD TO THE NEWLY REVISED EDITION

I first met Julianne Bochinski when she was a freshman in my science class at Mary Immaculate Academy in the fall of 1981. Julianne, like her fellow students, knew that one of the major curricula requirements toward achieving a grade in my science class was to complete a science fair project. Through the years my announcement of the science fair project assignment has usually been met with sighs of dismay as students realize that a science project is no small task. However, Julianne's enthusiasm for the assignment, as well as the enthusiasm of her classmates, was remarkably strong from the outset. The energy and dedication that this class gave to the science fair was like none I had ever seen before. There was a feeling of excitement in the air, and I knew that something special was happening. Julianne's topic was "Alcohol as a Fuel: Recycling Wastes into Energy." Her project, along with four other projects from my science class, became winning science projects at the 1982 Connecticut Science Fair. It was a year to remember. These five students together received the state trophy for representing the most outstanding school in the state for 1982.

I will never forget the events of that year, which inspired many talented and creative students in following years and, perhaps, paved the way to Julianne's journey into the world of science. She continued to volunteer her time to the Connecticut Science Fair after graduating from high school and afforded young people the opportunities that she experienced when she was a science fair contestant.

It is a known fact that students who do science fair projects and are exposed to science fair participation tend to develop valuable skills such as analytical thinking and creative problem solving. These tools assist them in dealing with real-life situations. Not everyone will become a scientist, but this exposure will broaden their horizons and lead them to other worthwhile pursuits.

This book is a great resource not only for students but more important for teachers and parents who encourage and guide young people throughout their formative years. Julianne's journey took her along many avenues from studying science to becoming an attorney and author, both of which are rooted in the scientific field. Perhaps one day an idea germinating from this book will take a budding young scientist on an incredible journey of a profound and amazing discovery that leads to a Nobel Prize.

God's blessings,

Sister Mary Christine Jachowdik, D.M.
Assistant Fair Director and Member of
the Board of Directors for the Connecticut
Science Fair

ACKNOWLEDGMENTS

I would like to express my grateful appreciation to the many people who have touched my life by offering their support and assistance to make this revised edition possible. As with the first edition, I remain indebted to Sister Mary Christine, Assistant Fair Director and member of the Board of Directors of the Connecticut Science Fair Association, for her assistance in selecting the 50 award-winning science fair projects that appear in Part II. She also brightens the days of many students across the country who write me with queries about their science fair projects. As past chairman of the mathematics department at the former Mary Immaculate Academy in New Britain, Connecticut, Sister Mary Christine has mentored science students for almost 30 years.

Acknowledgment is also due Science Service, Inc., in Washington, D.C., for providing me with listings of the state, regional, and foreign science fairs. As a nonprofit institution, Science Service has been dedicated to providing education programs in science for students around the world since 1921.

I also wish to thank the people at John Wiley & Sons, Inc., who have made my job easier. many thanks are due Kate Bradford, my editor, for her insight and for the opportunity to produce the revised edition.

Finally, I wish to thank my parents, Edmund and Elizabeth Bochinski, who have always been there to support me.

Student Consultants

A very talented group of young scientists deserves an extra special acknowledgment for their ideas and input into the science fair projects that appear in Part II. These students are:

- Eduardo Federico Canedo, "Does the Period of Motion of a Pendulum Depend on Its Weight, Amplitude, or Length?"
- Alexander Caravaca, "Does a Golf Ball's Bounciness Influence the Distance That It Will Travel?"

- Andrea Marie Caravaca, "Measuring the Brightness of an Incandescent Light Bulb"
- George F. Claffey, "What Section of a Town Has the Most Pollution in the Form of Airborne Particles?"
- Amy Concilio, "What Colored Dyes Are Found in Powdered Drink Mix and Colored Marking Pens?"
- Brian J. Curtin, "Are Your Clams Safe to Eat?"
- Kirsten B. Glass, "How Effective Is Lobster Shell Chitin in Filtering Wastewater Metallic Ions?"
- Michelle Harris, "Polarization and Stress Analysis of Airplane Windows"
- Kristin Hertzig, "Are Dogs Colorblind?"
- Adam K. Horelik, "Do All Plants Transpire at the Same Rate under Different Sources of Light?"
- Sara Horesco, "What Colored Dyes Are Found in Powdered Drink Mix and Colored Markers?"
- David A. Karanian, "The Relationship between Alcohol Dosage and Dependency in a Rat"
- Albert Kim, "Which Angle of Attack Generates the Most Lift?"
- Theresa Konicki, "How Can the Amount of Bacteria Found on Kitchen Sponges and Dishcloths Be Reduced?"
- Iwona Korza, "The Great American Lawn and Pristine Water: Can They Coexist?"
- Kasia Koziol-Dube, "Can Food Molds Be Used to Reduce Bacteria Spread by a Pet Rabbit?"
- Cathy Magliocco, "Can Limestone Be Used to Protect Pine Trees from Acid Rain?"
- Jodi Marak, "How Does Acid Rain Affect the Cell Structure of *Spirogyra*?"
- Kathy Mikk, "How Does Saltwater Mix in an Estuary?"
- Meredith Miller, "The Effects of Gender Identity on Short-Term Memory"
- Christina L. Olson, "Environmental Effects on the Biodegradability of Plastic Bags, Paper Bags, and Newspaper"
- Sarah Ann Pacyna, "The Physics of Cheating in Baseball"
- Celeste N. Peterson, "Can the Heartbeat of a Chicken Embryo Be Detected without Breaking Its Eggshell?"
- Mira Rho, "How Effective Are Various Items in Protecting against Ultraviolet Radiation?"
- Jason Riha, "Are Composites of Wood Stronger than Solid Wood?"
- Laura Sharpe, "What Is the Effect of #6 Heating Oil on *Elodea densa* in an Aquatic Environment?"
- Christina Smilnak, "Can Plant Cloning Be Used Effectively by Produce Growers?"

- Robert Smith, "An Analysis of the Bacteria and Heavy Metal Content of Sewage before and after Treatment at a Sewage Plant"
- Margaret Stanek, "How Effective Is Beta Carotene in Fighting Cancer in Plants?"
- Karen Thickman, "The Effect of Electromagnetic Fields on *Eremosphaera* Algae Cells"
- Connie W. Tsao, "Shape and Viscous Effect"
- Betsy Ruth Velasco, "What Substance Is Most Effective for Preventing the Breeding of Bacteria in Waterbeds?"
- Christopher Waluk, "Footwear versus Bacteria"
- Frank Waluk, "Can Earthworms Be Used to Recycle Kitchen Wastes into Fertile Garden Soil?" and "Are Dandelions as Effective as Commonly Prescribed Antibiotics against Bacteria?"
- John Wasielewski, "What Would Happen to Climate, Weather Patterns, and Life Forms if the Earth Were Cubical?"
- Joseph Wasielewski, "Can the Life Span of a Soap Bubble Be Extended in Different Temperatures and Atmospheric Conditions?" and "Can Mathematical Patterns Be Found in Johann Sebastian Bach's Two-Movement Preludes and Fugues?"
- Michael M. Wasielewski, "Do Gas Stations Affect the Soil Around Them?"

International Science and Engineering Fair Alumni

- Nicole D. D'Amato, "The Presence of Heavy Metals in a Coastal Body of Water and Their Effect on Aquatic Life"

- Matthew Green, "The Wave, the Golden Mean, and $r = \left[\dfrac{2}{\left(-1 + \sqrt{5} \right)} \right]^{\wedge} \theta$"

- Damon O. Kheir-Eldin, "Improving the Antibacterial Effects of Garlic"
- Katherine Frances Orzel, "The P-Trap: A Bacteria Cauldron" and "The P-Trap: A Continuing Dilemma"

SI (METRIC) CONVERSION TABLE

Both the English and the SI (metric) systems of measurement have been used in this book to simplify the student's understanding of specialized experimental procedures and the measurement-specific scientific instruments discussed.

	English	Symbol =	SI (Metric)	Symbol
Length	1 inch	in.	2.54 centimeters	cm
	1 foot	ft.	30.40 centimeters	cm
	1 yard	yd.	0.90 meter	m
	1 mile	mi.	1.60 kilometers	km
Mass	1 ounce	oz.	28.00 grams	g
	1 pound	lb.	0.45 kilogram	kg
Volume	1 teaspoon	tsp.	5.00 milliliters	ml
	1 tablespoon	tbsp.	15.00 milliliters	ml
	1 fluid ounce	fl. oz.	30.00 milliliters	ml
	1 cup	c.	0.24 liter	l
	1 pint	pt.	0.47 liter	l
	1 quart	qt.	0.95 liter	l
	1 gallon	gal.	3.80 liters	l

Temperature

Water freezes at:

32 degrees Fahrenheit	°F	0 degrees Celsius	°C

Water boils at:

212 degrees Fahrenheit		100 degrees Celsius	

Normal human body temperature:

98.6 degrees Fahrenheit		37 degrees Celsius	

To convert Fahrenheit to Celsius:

$$(°F - 32) \times {}^5\!/_9$$

To convert Celsius to Fahrenheit:

$$\frac{°C}{{}^5\!/_9} + 32$$

INTRODUCTION

I have to laugh when I read the introduction I wrote to the last edition of this book. I wrote it during the early to mid-1990s when it seemed as though science fairs and science projects had gone as far as they possibly could go. Everyone in the field thought that science fairs had moved to the ultimate level of sophistication in 1993 with the implementation of various rules that govern the protocol a student must follow before attempting to perform certain forms of scientific research, or when science fair exhibitions evolved into poster sessions where the display of many different subject matter became obsolete, or when students had begun to seriously use computers in the presentation of their project data and results. Those of us involved in science fair administration at that time thought that these advancements meant that science fairs had reached the final frontier. What else could possibly change or be improved upon? Well, that was nine years ago, which now seems like the dinosaur age in terms of how far technology, science fairs, and science fair projects have evolved to date.

Nine years ago, most of us were new to this thing called the Internet and some of us didn't even know what it was. Nine years ago, yours truly thought she had reached the cutting edge of technology when I purchased a "state-of-the-art" Macintosh Performa 450 PC computer that ran at a whopping speed of 25 MHz. When I realized that this "superfast" model couldn't dial up effectively into the fast-moving would of the Internet, this fabulous piece of machinery quickly became a heaping pile of junk, which lead to many more "state-of-the-art-become-pile-of-junk" computers to follow. And, nine years ago, top science fair project participants usually received only a nice trophy, a modest gift, or a dinner prize for their achievement. Well, what a difference nine years make. Today, many of you don't even remember a world without the Internet, much less a personal computer. And the rewards for science fair excellence? Well, let's just say that the economic incentives and opportunities are so incredible now that you cannot afford to pass up a chance to participate in your local, state, or regional science fair.

Science fairs of the new millennium are prestigious annual conventions for exchanging ideas and technologies among students of all interests and backgrounds. Science fairs are a fun way to gain valuable science experience, and they also provide perhaps what will be the only opportunity you will get as a student to learn what it will be like to work in the real world as an adult. That is, you will need to acquire various skills that have nothing at all to do with science such as making contacts, networking, preparing a tradeshow-like display, and public speaking. Science fairs provide an incredible learning experience that will reward you handsomely, not only in the present moment, but also when you apply for college admission and beyond.

Over the past year I have had the opportunity to attend a number of state and regional science fairs throughout the United States and the Intel International Science and Engineering Fair. As a result of my travels and the suggestions made by many students, teachers, judges, and fair directors I interviewed, I have thoroughly updated each of the introductory chapters and all the appendixes to provide you with timely and useful information (including Web site links to key resources where applicable) to guide you through each and every phase of creating, submitting, and presenting your science fair project. Once again, this edition still contains the original 50 award-winning science fair project outlines that have come from real students who have won awards for their work. And once again, I have to caution you that these outlines are merely recipes that you are encouraged to sample and not duplicate in place of your own project. As such, just because these students have won awards for these projects does not mean that the outlines are guaranteed to work for you in accordance with the procedures given, nor are you guaranteed to win an award by following any of these outlines. To this end, the results of the projects have been purposely eliminated and substituted by questions for you to think about and to give you an example of how to observe, analyze, and draw conclusions for your own project. The projects are provided only to give you an idea of the methodology behind the scientific method (see chapter 2) after which you should model your project or to spark an idea for a different science fair project. Since many first-time science fair participants reading this book have never had the opportunity to visit a science fair to see what a science project involves, the outlines are also a way to bring the science fair home to them. These outlines show a range of skills and techniques, from those used in simple projects for young readers to those used in sophisticated projects that have competed at the Intel International Science and Engineering Fair. Once again, take a look at the projects for inspiration and guidance but do not copy a project for your own. You will rob yourself of a wonderful learning experience. Nobody wins if a project is copied straight out of a book.

I want to conclude by saying that while a great many books on the subject of science fair projects have been written to help students and their parents "survive the challenge" of completing a science fair project, the purpose of this book and its prior editions has always been to present a clear and comprehensive format for completing a project in a way that will help students and their parents see the challenge as a wonderful opportunity for achievement. I hate to say it, but the whole process can become a self-fulfilling prophecy. That is, if you approach your science fair project assignment in a negative frame of mind, there is no doubt that your project will become an ordeal for you. But, if you approach it with an open mind and a positive outlook as to what you will learn, who you will meet, and where it might take you, you will be pleasantly surprised to see how gratifying the whole experience is, especially now in the new era of science fairs. Everything you need to get started and move forward through each phase of your project is here in this newly updated revision. I hope that the tips, examples, and references contained in these pages will open your mind to the endless possibilities that await you as you make your way through the process of completing, submitting, and presenting an award-winning science fair project. Enjoy the journey!

PART

I

A Complete Guide to Science Fair Projects

1

SCIENCE FAIRS AND SCIENCE FAIR PROJECTS

What Is a Science Fair Project?

A science fair project is different from any other type of project you work on at school. Why? Because it is an independent educational activity that encompasses a variety of skills, many of which you have to teach yourself as you go along. A science fair project gives you hands-on experience and knowledge in your own independent field of study involving science, math, or engineering. It is a challenging extracurricular assignment that allows you to use your own ideas or a topic that you develop with your science instructor to investigate a scientific problem or question that interests you. You will not only be learning about a specific field of science and perhaps acquiring a unique skill in this field, but getting to know what it would be like to work in this field as an adult.

For example, you will learn how to investigate, network, conduct interviews, follow rules and guidelines, use various tools and equipment, analyze data, draft an abstract, write a report, prepare a display, and speak in public. With work and dedication on your part, the experience you will gain and the skills you will achieve from this extraordinary activity will be well worth all the time you put into it. The reason is plain and simple: as you make progress and begin to see your project develop and come together, your self-esteem will soar, and the project that was initially such a challenge, will eventually become a grand personal achievement—unique only to you.

What Is a Science Fair?

Every spring, thousands of students in grades 5–12 prepare science fair projects for competitions held by school districts, counties, and states. These fairs are public exhibitions of the students' projects to recognize their work and to stimulate interest in science. Professionals from the scientific community often judge the science projects. Students who participate can earn valuable experience along with educational grants, scholarships, and other prizes. Additionally, many college recruiters give science fair project participation high marks in considering an application for college admission.

Every year, thousands of students enter state, regional, or foreign affiliate science fairs of the Intel International Science and Engineering Fair like this recent state fair in Massachusetts.

When you participate in a local science fair, you have a chance to move on to a higher level of competition in a state or regional science fair. Today, most regional and state science fairs are charter affiliated with the Intel International Science and Engineering Fair (ISEF), which is considered the World Series of science fairs. (See Appendix D for a complete listing of state, regional, and foreign science fairs currently affiliated with Intel ISEF.) The grand finale of all state and regional science fairs in the United States and in several other countries is the Intel International Science and Engineering Fair (Intel ISEF).

The Intel ISEF is sponsored by Intel Corporation and several other major companies and organizations and is administered by Science Service, Inc., a national, nonprofit group based in Washington, D.C. In addition to the Intel ISEF, Science Service administers the Discovery Channel Young Scientist Challenge (for middle school students) and the very prestigious Intel Science Talent Search (formerly called the Westinghouse Science Talent Search) for high school students. These events are considered to be the most prestigious competitions in precollege science. (For more information about the Discovery Channel Young Scientist Challenge or the Intel Science Talent Search and other notable science fair project competitions, see Appendix E.) Science Service also offers wonderful programs and publications, including the weekly publication *Science News*.

What Is the Intel International Science and Engineering Fair (Intel ISEF)?

According to Science Service, the nonprofit organization that has administered this event for over 50 years, the Intel ISEF is the only international science fair project competition for students in grades 9–12 in the world. The top high school students from each Intel ISEF–affiliated fair are invited to compete at this prestigious convention, which is held annually in a major city, usually in the United States. The fair welcomes about 1,200 contestants, on average, from nearly 40 different countries. To see if there is a state or regional Intel ISEF–affiliated science fair near you, see Appendix D.

The Intel ISEF is, in a word, incredible! You would be awed by the sheer magnitude of this event, which hosts the finest science fair projects in the world, displayed by exhibitors from every part of the globe, many of whom come dressed in their finest suits or school uniforms. These exhibitors are often accompanied by an entourage of mentors, teachers, and families eagerly snapping photos and waving flags at awards ceremonies. Along with the exhibitors, there is an impressive group of Intel ISEF associates and judges who make up a Who's Who list in various scientific fields.

It is a scene like no other, except perhaps the Olympic games, and this is not an exaggeration. The annual event is a weeklong affair complete with opening and closing ceremonies, formal parties, awards presentations, workshops, networking meetings, sight-seeing tours, and of course intense judging rounds. Exhibitors compete for over $2 million in college scholarships, tuition grants, internships, and ultimately (for the top grand prize winners) a chance to attend the Nobel Prize ceremonies in Stockholm, Sweden.

When you consider the opportunities Intel ISEF presents—meeting students who will be tomorrow's scientific leaders, networking with the best minds in science, gaining exposure to the scientific community, and possibly winning awards (some of which could pay your entire college tuition for four years)—your science fair project is sure to take on a whole new meaning to you. I wish you great success on your project. Perhaps someday you too may be invited to attend Intel ISEF as a contestant. It is the experience of a lifetime.

If you would like more information about the Intel ISEF, the Intel Science Talent Search, the Discovery Channel Young Scientist Challenge, or an affiliated fair in your area, please write to:

Science Service, Inc.
1719 N Street, N.W.
Washington, DC 20036
Phone: (202) 785-2255
Fax: (202) 785-1243
E-mail: sciedu@sciserv.org
Internet: www.sciserv.org

The Intel ISEF Guidelines

If you've read up to this point, you might be wondering if your local county, state, regional, or country science fair is affiliated with the Intel ISEF. Chances are that it is. Therefore, the focus of this book is on creating, developing, experimenting, and presenting a top-notch science fair project according to the Intel ISEF rules and guidelines. The following sections are organized according to the steps that you should take in preparing a science fair project for such a fair.

2
BEFORE YOU GET STARTED

Basic Issues to Consider before Starting Your Project

Because you may be doing a science fair project for the very first time, you need to learn the basic parts of a science fair project (namely, the **scientific method**).

The Scientific Method

A science project studies a scientific problem in order to answer a proposed question or develop a better technique or final product. Science projects primarily involve research and tests to arrive at a specific conclusion. The basic procedure involved in a science project is modeled on a process called the **scientific method.** This method consists of the following elements: problem/purpose, hypothesis, research/procedure, experiment, and analysis of results or conclusion. The following list defines each element of the scientific method and provides a basic example of how you would develop a topic through the scientific method.

The Scientific Method by Example

Problem/Purpose: The problem or question for which you are testing or seeking to solve.

Example: Does an interrupted sleeping pattern or disturbed circadian rhythm affect one's alertness?

Hypothesis: Your educated guess about the solution to the problem and the results you expect to achieve from your experiment.

Example: I believe that sleep influences one's alertness and that an interrupted sleeping pattern or disturbed circadian rhythm would negatively affect one's alertness.

(Continued)

Research/Procedure: The process by which you gather information. This may include consulting reference materials, the Internet, mentors or professionals in the scientific field you are studying, or other persons or organizations related to your subject who will help you understand your topic and help you formulate how you will test your hypothesis through an experiment. At this stage you should carefully plan how the experiment will be carried out through time frames, variables, and controls, and how the results will be observed and measured.

> *Example:* You may start with the premise that two groups of people will be studied. Group I will be allowed to sleep 9 hours without interruption. Group II will be allowed to sleep 10 hours but will be awakened every 2 hours for 15 minutes to give group members a total of 9 hours of sleep. Following the periods of sleep, both groups will be tested for alertness to determine whether their performance is influenced by the conditions to which they were subjected prior to the test.

As you continue through this stage you will need to keep fine-tuning your proposed experimental plan.

> *Example:* What materials or subjects will you use to conduct your experiment? Will you account for variables such as age, gender, daily routine, amount of food consumed during the day, daily exercise routines, and so on? Do you plan to measure alertness through a written test that measures cognitive performance? Or do you plan to measure alertness through a physical reflex test? Finally, how many trials of your experiment will you conduct and how will you collect and analyze your data?

Experiment: The process by which you carry out the procedure you outlined during the research/procedure stage to test your hypothesis.

Analysis and Conclusions: The solution to your proposed question and proof or rejection of your hypothesis.

> *Example:* Based on the data from this test, interrupted sleepers perform less efficiently than noninterrupted ones on an alertness test.

You will want to explain how the results may have varied among different conditions, subjects, and trials, as well as the value of your research. You may be able to suggest ways to improve the problem or experiment for future study. Finally, you may conclude by explaining the practical results and usefulness of your study.

> *Example:* The results of this experiment varied between subjects of different ages, genders, and lifestyles but overall provide a similar conclusion: an interrupted sleeping pattern or disturbed circadian rhythm does affect one's alertness, both mentally and physically, which can become a serious problem over time. A more detailed study could be conducted to further refine the results. This project has important implications for professionals with interrupted sleep patterns, such as emergency medical technicians, doctors, and firefighters, who perform critical work and are often subjected to interrupted sleeping patterns.

Going Solo or Teaming Up

Before we move ahead to finding a great topic and getting started with it, you will need to decide whether you are going to work on your project alone or as part of a team with a fellow student or students. Most projects produced for science fair competition are by individual entrants. A smaller percentage are by team entrants and there is a very good reason for that. Team projects require joint commitment, shared interest, and a balanced work ethic from both partners, along with great interpersonal skills that will last over a period of time. Finding two or three students who match all these qualities is not easy. Team projects can be very rewarding, but they are not for everyone. There are pros and cons to working with another student and you need to examine them carefully and make sure you are teaming up for the right reasons before you decide to commit to a team project.

Positive Reasons to Team Up

Many a scientist and engineer will tell you that in the real world they often have to work together with their peers as part of a team on a research project because each member of the team contributes a valuable skill or area of expertise

These talented young ladies' joint efforts worked so well that they not only won a trip to the Intel ISEF, but they also earned top awards in their category. Evening gowns? You bet! Besides an intense round of project interviews, the Intel ISEF also features many other activities, including a lavish formal dinner party for its international contestants.

different from the others. The synergy of the unique qualities of each team member creates a successful research or engineering project. Similarly, if you and a fellow student have complementary skills that would be useful on a given topic, a team project might be a great thing for both of you. For example, if both you and a partner are interested in a topic that requires biochemistry laboratory skills in which you have some experience or skill, and it also requires meticulous data collection and mathematical analysis skills, which your friend is a whiz at, it would be a shame to not collaborate with this person as a prospective partner.

Reasons Not to Team Up

Keep in mind that you are going to be working with your partner for several months or more. While you may be on the same side of the fence today, you may be on opposite sides in a short period of time, especially if one of you is doing all the work. Be sure you are teaming up with someone you can trust to work hard and be devoted to the best outcome of the science fair project. Do not team up with someone for the sole reason that he or she is your best friend or because you would like to be friends with him or her. While it is absolutely essential to work with someone you like and get along with (remember, you're both going to be tied into this project for a long time), it can be burdensome and destructive in the long run if you and your friend have a disagreement and take it personally. Both of you need to set some ground rules before you embark on a project together. Make sure that you agree on your joint responsibilities and duties to the project ahead of time, and make a pact that you will not let your friendship get in the way of the project or the other way around!

Summary

1. In its basic form, a science fair project is made up of a series of steps or a formula called the scientific method. Almost all science fair projects fit within the framework of the scientific method.

2. The scientific method consists of the following steps: problem/purpose, hypothesis, research/procedure, experiment, and analysis of results or conclusion.

3. Most science fair projects are conducted by individual students. However, a science fair project can also be a team effort. Before you get started on your project, you will need to know whether you will be going solo or working as part of a team. Be sure to consider the pros and cons of going forward with a team project before signing up for one.

3

GETTING STARTED

Select a Topic

Once you understand the foundation of a science fair project and how it works, it is time to select a topic for your own science fair project.

Believe it or not, selecting a topic for a science fair project may be the toughest part of the process. Every year many students planning to do a science fair project begin an unorganized search of the public library or the Internet through volumes and volumes of scientific articles and the latest scientific news stories without knowing what they are looking for. After several useless attempts at finding a subject to work on, most students become overwhelmed and frustrated. The Internet and public library are good places to find a topic, but most students are not focused when they begin their search. Without knowing what it is that you are looking for, it is almost impossible for you to come up with something that is going to work as a topic. The key is to have some direction before you begin. This chapter will help you select a topic that is both interesting and meaningful to you by showing you how to approach the selection process in a focused way.

Primary Areas for Finding a Topic: Your Interests, Experiences, and Resources

The first step in the process of selecting a topic is simple but extremely important: pick an area of science in which you have some particular interest, experience, or resources available to you. You may wonder if this is really necessary, especially if your science fair project is a required part of your science class grade for the semester. You may think that any project topic will do as long as it helps you to make the grade. If you are thinking this way, please think again. Even if you did not choose to do a science fair project, picking a topic that you are interested in or know something about is really important! There are several reasons why. First, you are going to be with your project topic for quite possibly a few months or longer. If you don't pick the right topic, you will be bored stiff! Second, if you want to do a top-notch job, you will need to choose something that you can feel passionate about. It's guaranteed to be reflected in your work. Third, you are going to have to live the life of a dedicated researcher for a period of time. If you don't have any idea what kind of work the project entails, you won't get very far. "A Study of the Applications of Single Crystal Carbon Nanotubes" may sound like a winning topic, but if you know absolutely nothing about this subject, have no experience with this area of science, and do not have the materials or resources to help you with this topic (see "Find a Good Mentor" later in this chapter), it's probably not going to work for you. Do yourself a favor and look closely at your interests, experience, and resources before settling on a topic. And remember, there is nothing worse than being unhappy with your topic and feeling like you're stuck with it. Do not be afraid to get out of it and find another topic if you do happen to become bored or disinterested with your original idea.

Think about Your Interests

One suggestion to help you in approaching your topic is to make a list of general science categories that you really like. Then go through your list and classify each category into subcategories of interest. For example, if one of the categories you listed was *medicine and health,* some subcategories might include *nutrition, diet,* and perhaps *vitamin supplements.* Chances are good that you will find yourself more interested in one area of science than another. Such preferences usually indicate good possibilities for topics. If, for example, you chose *vitamin supplements* as your subject, you should then try to identify a particular aspect of this subject that you want to investigate. For example, do you want to study the effects of plant compounds known as *polyphenols* in inhibiting the damaging effects of free radicals, or do you want to see how they interact with certain over-the-counter drugs? If one of the categories you listed was *zoology,* some subcategories might include *wildlife, birds,* and *environmental conditions affecting their lives.* If you chose *environmental conditions affecting the life of birds,* you should determine whether you want to study something like the atmospheric conditions that influence their migration, or how atmospheric conditions affect their life span. These are just a few examples of how you would develop a topic from your selected subject area. For more lists of scientific categories and subcategories that can be broken down into topics, see Appendix A.

Remember, your best choice for a topic is a subject in which you have a particular interest. While it is helpful to have some knowledge of the topic before you choose it, this is not essential. Unless you pick a topic that is very challenging, if you are interested and resourceful, you will learn what you need to know.

Think about Your Experiences

Another way to select a topic is to examine your past experiences. Do you have any skills or experience in a particular area of science? For example, perhaps you dismantled your personal computer to troubleshoot a problem and noticed that the microprocessor was rather hot. Perhaps you wondered if the heat would be detrimental to the microprocessor or if there was some type of device or material inside your computer that protected the microprocessor from the heat. Your curiosity might have led you to read about *heat sinks,* which are designed to draw heat from microprocessors. As you read about heat sinks you might have wondered if the metal composition of a heat sink would affect its ability to draw the most heat. Such an experience makes an excellent example of how you would derive a topic from a past experience.

Another way to find a topic from past experiences is to recall any unusual experiences you have had. For example, perhaps you once felt that your eyesight sharpened whenever you ate a certain vegetable, or perhaps you discovered a rare type of moss growing on a tree stump in your backyard that repelled insects. You may have wondered whether the material that enabled your watch dial to glow in the dark also emitted radiation that was affecting your environment. Or, you might remember personal experiences that lead you to investigate or conduct research because the subject was near and dear to you. For example, perhaps your beloved pet cat developed *feline fatty liver disease,* an often fatal disease for cats that usually does not show any symptoms until it is too late to treat. Your difficult experience with your pet cat might have led you to research the subject to see how you could help your cat, and it may have provided you with the opportunity to work closely with your family veterinarian in the diagnosis and treatment of your cat. Personal experiences such as these are excellent sources for project ideas.

Tap into Your Resources

While thinking about your interests and past experiences, do not forget the personal resources you have at your disposal. They are excellent to consult for a topic and can become very instrumental to you as you progress through your science fair project. So think about people you know and how they might be able to assist you in finding your topic. In the example of the *feline fatty liver disease,* such an experience might have fostered a good relationship with the family veterinarian, an excellent personal resource to consult about developing a zoological science idea into a science fair project topic. In the example, the family veterinarian might be able to assist you in your study and testing of *feline fatty liver disease.* The great thing about personal resources is that they are all around you and their advice is free (hopefully). These individuals do not have to be scientists, engineers, or doctors in order for you to tap into their background and find a great topic. For example, start in your own home. What does your mom or dad do professionally? If your dad works in building and construction, he might be a great resource for a topic that would investigate something like the durability of concrete. As you talk more and more with him about this subject you may be able to develop a topic such as *the effects of spray-coated fiber reinforcement on the strength of concrete.* If your cousin is an accomplished violinist, he or she might be a great resource for a topic that would investigate *instrument sound quality, pitch,* and so on. As you talk to him about the subject, you might come up with a topic such as *the effects of rosin on the sound quality of a violin.* If your next-door neighbor works for your state's department of transportation, he might make an excellent resource for a topic that might investigate traffic patterns, traffic lights, and rush hour traffic, which could lead to a topic in this area. Personal resources, such as family, friends, and professional contacts, can help you to find a great topic.

Secondary Areas for Finding a Topic: Scientific Abstracts, the Internet, Traditional Periodicals, and Current and Local Topics of Interest

Research Scientific Abstracts

Another possible source for a good topic is scientific abstracts. Abstracts can be located in bound scientific journals that are usually available at your local college or university library. These specialized journals are used primarily by science professionals. Articles are generally grouped into two classes: research experimental reports and reviews of scientific literature. Monthly issues are published in accordance with a cumulative subject and author index that is published annually. But remember, if you look through scientific abstracts, be sure to examine them in a field of study that you are interested in.

Research the Internet and Electronic Periodicals

Since so many great Web sites come and go over a short period of time, it was not feasible to list all of the great science fair topic idea Web sites online at the time this book was written. However, the 10 Web sites and electronic scientific magazines listed on the following page have great content and have been online for a while, so we hope they will still be around by the time you read this. They offer terrific resources and ideas that you can use to generate a science fair topic.

Research Magazines and Other Traditional Periodicals

Another area to investigate if you have not already thought of a topic is the periodical literature in your field of interest. Go to your local library and look through the most recent magazines and newsletters in the field you have chosen. These are effective aids in finding and researching a topic because they are concise and up-to-date. Magazines such as *National Geographic* (www.nationalgeographic.com), *Discover Magazine* (www.discover.com), *Popular Science* (www.popsci.com/popsci), *Popular Mechanics* (www. popularmechanics.com), *Mother Earth News* (www.motherearthnews.com), *Scientific American* (www.scientificamerican.com), and *Prevention* (www. prevention.com) and most computer and technology magazines are the best traditional journals to consult while searching for an original topic.

Research Current Topics or Local Topics of Interest

Keep in mind, too, that a successful project tends to be one that works with a new technology, problem, issue of current interest, or a novel approach to an ongoing problem. For example, back in the late 1970s and early 1980s, the main concern of many Americans was the energy crisis issue, so projects that involved energy themes fared well at that time. In the 1990s and even today, environmental issues remain popular. And now, in the new millennium, many students have been interested in projects with themes concerning all aspects of wireless communications, antibiotic-resistant bacteria, urban planning problems, and medicine and health issues. A good place to look up current issues or technologies is America Online. Just type in the key words "health," "science," or "computers" and you will retrieve many recent news articles in these subject areas that can be helpful in finding a topic that is related to a subject of popular current interest. Also, while browsing America Online be sure to check out the key word "science fair." It brings up some helpful content and advice for doing a science fair project and includes a few message boards where you can interact with other students to get ideas or advice for your science fair project.

Often, a successful science fair project works with a technology or issue of popular current interest, or a novel approach to an ongoing problem.

Another area to tap into is your own backyard. Certain topics and problems are ideal for your geographic location. For example, a review of science fair projects at a current regional science fair in Texas revealed that some projects focused on issues relating to oil refineries, weather, and space science, while at a recent Florida regional fair, projects dealt with the eradication of insects, marine and aquatic sciences, and agriculture. These geographically localized areas of science can provide some terrific topics that may be ideal for you in terms of your location, whereas they might not be as ideal for students located elsewhere. Take advantage of where you live and your local resources.

Other Areas for Finding a Topic: Local, State, or Regional Science Fairs, and Science Fair Workshops

One of the best ways to get ideas is to surround yourself with them. If you are still having trouble finding a science fair project topic, try visiting a local school, regional, or state science fair. If you cannot get to the science fair in person, turn to Appendix B in the back of this book, which contains a list of over one hundred actual science fair project titles taken from award-winning science fair projects at a variety of recent state and regional Intel ISEF–affiliated science fairs. The topics are broken down by Intel ISEF categories of science. Or log on to the

This exhibitor at the Delaware Valley Science Fair literally found his science fair project in his backyard!

Internet and visit some of the Intel ISEF–affiliated science fair Web sites that are listed in Appendix D. You will get to see the quality of science fair project work performed by middle school and high school students at some of these Web sites, as well as what topics are current and interesting to you.

Attend a Science Fair Workshop

Many state and regional science fairs hold workshops for students during the summer and fall to help students understand the science fair project process overall, as well to show them how to focus in on a particular scientific field and

A word of caution: While it is beneficial to visit a local, state, or regional science fair to see what a winning science fair project looks like and to get ideas, do not attend a science fair for the purpose of copying another student's work. Not only would this be plagiarism, but you would not achieve success by showing up at the following year's science fair with the identical project that won at a previous year's fair. Science fair administrators and judges will easily remember a winning entry from a previous fair and would possibly disqualify your entry if they sense you copied another student's work.

narrow it down into a specific scientific question or problem for the upcoming year's science fair. Many of these workshops offer smaller sessions in various fields of science, mathematics, and engineering. By attending one of these workshops, not only will you be able to develop your science fair project topic, but, you will have the opportunity to meet some valuable contacts. You could even find a mentor to guide you in your research, and perhaps assist you in accessing valuable testing equipment or the facilities of a research laboratory. More information about working with a mentor appears later in this chapter.

Organize Your Investigation

Once you have found an area of science or a subject that satisfies you, you are ready to get started. At this time, it is necessary to organize yourself and take inventory. You can begin by getting a notebook to create a journal of everything you will be learning and doing for your project. A journal is the best way to organize your research, and what's more, it will serve as an excellent outline for your report. In your journal describe articles you have read, places you have visited, data results, and other points you think are worth noting. Write down important information so that you will not have to search through your references again.

Next, take into consideration the amount of time you have to complete the project, so that you can plan accordingly. As a researcher, you are investigating a particular problem or question. It would be helpful to know exactly what you are aiming for and how far you are willing to go to pursue your immediate objective. In addition to time constraints, you will need to take note of rules and guidelines established by your regional or state science fair, the contacts you will need to make, the resources and mentors you are going to need, supplies and equipment you will require, and finally the expenses you will incur.

Budget Your Time and Projected Expenses

Realize what you are getting into. Most science fairs are held from late February through late April. If you have been assigned to a science fair project by your teacher, you probably will know about the assignment as early as the preceding fall semester. That means you will have four or five months to do your project. However, keep in mind that due to the Scientific Rule Committee (SRC) guidelines that almost all state and regional science fairs follow, you will need to have your project proposal and description forms filled out and ready for submission as early as the November or December prior to the science fair in order to get approval for the work you are planning to do. If this is the case, then you will need to have your project topic and plan for experimentation worked out well before the SRC deadline. When selecting a topic, be sure that you can reasonably make the contacts you need, perform your research, obtain the necessary materials and carry out your experimentation, and analyze your results within the amount of time you have. (See Chapter 4, "Define Your Objective," for more information on streamlining your topic into a feasible experiment.)

You should also look at the expenses that may arise for the type of project you have selected. You may be able to borrow various supplies, materials, and equipment from your school, or you may be eligible to work at a university or laboratory that will donate their equipment and supplies; however, there are some supplies that you may have to purchase. Consult with your parents, teacher, or mentor first to see how much can be budgeted for your project and if it is affordable prior to settling on your topic. For a list of scientific supply companies that can provide an estimate of costs for some of the supplies you may have to purchase, see Appendix C in the back of this book.

Project Limitations and Required Forms

First and foremost, rules established by the Intel ISEF will govern your research on your topic and experimentation. The Intel ISEF's Scientific Review Committee (SRC) continuously reviews and updates its rules out of concern for the safety and protection of student researchers and their advisers, as well as to comply with local and federal regulations governing research. Some of the areas in which strict rules apply involve vertebrate and nonvertebrate animals; human subjects; recombinant DNA; human and animal tissues; pathogenic agents, including bacteria, fungi, and molds; controlled substances and chemicals; mutagenic agents;

A Scientific Review Committee (SRC) establishes strict rules governing the handling of certain subject matter, such as in this project that studied fungus growth on amphibians linked to increased UV B radiation.

carcinogenic agents; infectious agents; and hazardous materials or devices. For projects involving those areas, you are required to complete additional forms for the prescreening of your project and approval by an Institutional Review Board authorized by your state or regional science fair prior to the start of your research. You should contact your state or regional fair director for a copy of your fair's specific rulebook and forms. (See Chapter 4 in this book for more information about getting your project approved. And see Appendix D in the back of this book for a list of science fairs across the United States and worldwide that are charter affiliates of the Intel ISEF. A copy of the Intel ISEF rule book can be obtained from Science Service, Inc., at the address listed in Chapter 1 of this book.)

Make Connections and Contacts

A good way to begin work on your topic is to check all relevant periodicals and scientific abstracts at your local library and on the Internet. Look for the names, addresses, phone numbers, and e-mail addresses of resources with whom you can get in touch before you begin to work on your project. The contact information you find may also supply cross-references and referrals to key people and places, such as scientists, engineers, technicians, universities, organizations, laboratories, and businesses. Take advantage of these helpful references because they are your best source for learning what you may need to do, where to go, and who to meet before you do anything else.

As soon as you think you have located some useful physical or e-mail addresses, write a letter to the sources you have found. State that you are a student working under a deadline, discuss the plans you have in mind for your project, and describe the information you will need to gather. Ask for all the available literature that your referral might be able to recommend on your topic, along with any suggestions or advice for your experimentation. Ask for additional references of people in your area who are working in this field and who might be able to serve as mentors or offer you a connection to an institution. Ask your referrals if they know of an institution that might be able to assist you by donating their facilities or equipment to help you carry out your research or experiment.

Make several copies of this letter and send them to the people, organizations, and businesses who may be able to help you. Many will be glad to help, especially if your topic relates to their own products, technologies, or ideas. Not only does it benefit then by fostering good public relations, but also, it may help to get their business name and products out in the public eye. Sending out such letters enables you to save time by eliminating useless searches and honing your information down to the details that you need. Remember, you can always refer to textbooks, periodicals, and scientific abstracts when you need additional information later on.

Included on the following pages are two letters. One was sent by a student requesting information on alcohol as an alternative energy resource. This letter resulted in four informational guides that helped the student through her entire project. Along with the guides, she received lists containing the titles of exclusive literature on her subject and the address of an alcohol fuel producer who lived in her own county who served as a good mentor. The other letter was sent out by another student requesting information on x-raying corked baseball bats. This letter also helped the student make contact with a helpful mentor, which is perhaps the best way to get started on your project. The last section of this chapter discusses the benefits of working with a mentor.

Find a Good Mentor

One of the best-kept secrets of students who have had a very successful science fair project experience is their affiliation with a mentor. These students have had the opportunity to work under the advice and guidance of a professional scientist or engineer. A mentor can help you in many ways in the planning of your project, including helping you obtain materials and supplies and possibly by enabling you to carry out your experimentation at a university, private corporation, or other testing facility. Students with a mentor often have a significant advantage over other students. This is especially the case at the high school level. If your goal is to make it to the top science fair competition in your state or to the Intel International Science and Engineering Fair, you really should consider making contact with a mentor.

Renewable Energy Information
P.O. Box 8900
Silver Spring, MD 20907

Dear Director:

I am a high school student currently working on a science project for my state's science fair. My project concerns the recycling of fermented organic garbage into ethyl alcohol. My objective is to see if it is possible for a household to construct a simple and inexpensive still capable of producing enough alcohol fuel to meet the household's energy needs. I also plan to compare ethyl alcohol with other natural fuel sources to determine its efficiency.

Recently, I found your address in an alcohol fuel directory. This guide mentioned that your organization would be able to assist ethyl alcohol fuel producers by providing them with suggestions and further information.

At this time, I would be grateful for any current information on alcohol production, still designs, and alcohol producers in my area. If possible, please send this information to me soon since I am working toward a February deadline.

If all goes well, this will be both an informative and stimulating project for me and my community.

Sincerely,

Student

Hillerich & Bradsby Company
P.O. Box 35700
Louisville, KY 40232-5700

Dear Sir:

I am an eighth grade student working on a science fair project that may be of interest to your company.

My project topic is "The Physics of Cheating in Baseball." Four bats were used to test my hypothesis which was that a baseball bat filled with sawdust, as opposed to a regular bat or bats filled with cork or rubber balls, will cause a baseball to travel the farthest on impact. I drilled out the center of three bats and filled one with sawdust, the second with rolled cork and the third with rubber balls. I left one bat alone to serve as a control. I tested the bats by placing each of them in a swinging device, which would hit a baseball placed on a batting tee when released. Out of the four bats, the sawdust-filled bat sent the baseball farther than the other bats.

In preparation for the State Science Fair, I would like to expand my project by seeing if it is possible to x-ray a baseball bat. I spoke with my doctor to find out if he or someone else would be willing to perform the X rays. He told me that I would have to find out whether a diagnostic machine X ray or metal fatigue/ stress fracture X ray would have to be performed. Please tell me which of these X rays would work with baseball bats.

Also, in doing my research I read an article, "The Physics of Foul Play" in *Discover,* in which tests were conducted at the request of MLB's Commissioner of Baseball. Do you have any information on how the bats were tested and what the results were? I would be grateful to have this information as soon as possible since I am working under a limited time frame. Thank you for your assistance.

Sincerely,

Student

Like all best-kept secrets and insider tips, a mentor is not easy to come by. To find a good mentor who works in the specific niche area of science to which your project pertains requires some effort, a little finesse, and a bit of luck on your part. Basically, the process involves networking, and that means you have to get out there and make connections through teachers, family, friends, and others before you will find that one person who will be a great resource to you and be willing to volunteer his or her time to work with you in the role of a mentor.

One way to make a connection with a mentor (if you do not have one through your school or family) would be to contact your local, state, or regional science fair. Many of these fairs have outreach programs for students that feature the volunteer support of professionals from the scientific community. Some science fairs have a very sophisticated program where you may have to file an application to qualify for a mentor since they usually have limited numbers of such individuals available. Additionally, a local university science department might be able to supply the name of a professor or graduate student who can help you. In any case, it is a good idea to try to seek out a mentor as soon as possible so that you will have enough time to discuss your project with that person, plan out the course of your research and experimentation, and get any necessary approvals.

Summary

1. Project topics can be found in a variety of different areas. Primary areas for finding a topic include focusing on your interests, experiences, and personal resources. Secondary areas for finding a topic include the Internet, traditional periodicals, scientific abstracts, and current and local topics of interest. Topics may also be found through visiting a local science fair or attending a science fair workshop.

2. Once you have found a topic that interests you, it is important to stop and analyze the feasibility of what you have chosen. Consider your time constraints, the rules and guidelines established by your regional or state science fair, the contacts you will need to make, the resources and mentors you are going to need, and finally, the expenses you will incur. Get a notebook to use as a journal in which you will record all your work.

3. Check all relevant periodicals and scientific abstracts at your local library and on the Internet for the names, addresses, phone numbers, and e-mail addresses of resources with whom you can get in touch before you begin to work on your project. Make contact with resources you have found in your research through writing letters or e-mails, making phone calls, and all other forms of networking.

4. Find a good mentor. Students with a mentor often have a significant advantage over other students. Finding a mentor requires networking with friends, family and others, so start looking early on in the process.

4

PLANNING AND CONDUCTING YOUR EXPERIMENT

The experiment can either make or break your science project. This is the backbone of the project, and you must put sufficient thought and preparation into it. You should plan to spend most of your time on a feasible experiment after researching. Your research should involve a practical application that includes measurements, analyses, or tests to answer a specific question. Judges look for these individual qualities and will be distracted if your project contains irrelevant facts and data.

Above all, make sure that the work you do follows the scientific method (see Chapter 2). Judges often see projects that are researched thoroughly and presented in a neat, attractive manner, only to find that they merely present a well-known idea, model, collection, or display that the public has seen too many times. Such exhibits are not experiments but mere demonstrations that do not merit high marks as science fair projects at the state and regional level. *Note however, that when working on an* **engineering project,** *you may in fact be constructing, designing, building, troubleshooting, or demonstrating a working model of a new product, a device to improve on an existing model or product, or an inventive model or device that addresses or solves an existing problem.* This is the nature of an engineering project and the judges expect it. However, even at the core of an engineering project there is a question or problem that is asked and addressed by the model, design, or device built.

In general, while preparing your project, try to present a question or problem and then prepare a series of tests to solve the problem or support a proposed hypothesis. If you follow the scientific method, your project should be easier to complete and will provide more meaningful results than if you do not use this method.

Because you want your results to be absolutely accurate, you should record all your data in your journal, regardless of whether or not they support your hypothesis. Your project will not be scored low or disqualified simply because your results did not support your hypothesis. You may develop your project by interpreting your end results and explaining why they were different from what you expected.

Keep in mind that judges do not expect you to come up with a revolutionary idea. They are more interested in seeing how much ingenuity and originality you

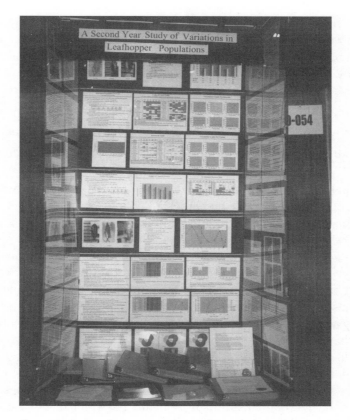

Some contestants continue to work on the same project for a second year's science fair because their original project experiment yielded results that opened new avenues of exploration for a second project study.

applied to an existing problem you are studying and the approach you took toward your problem. Most projects have been done before in one form or another. They usually differ to the extent that they are different approaches or applied techniques of an original idea or a confirmation of a conclusion under varying circumstances. Some contestants even submit the same project the following year at the same science fair because they have made significant progress in their topic since their first entry. Judges are mainly interested to see whether you chose the best method possible in your investigation, whether you have made the most effective use of materials, equipment, and techniques pertaining to your topic, and whether you have recorded and analyzed your data accurately and effectively.

Step One: Define Your Objective

Before you begin, streamline your proposed question. Decide what you want to prove, and try to attack the most important aspect of your topic. For example, if you chose oil spills as your topic, you would probably research its hazardous byproducts, cleanup solutions, and long-term effects on the environment. Such a broad topic would yield a variety of details without a specific focus or purpose. You must confine your topic to a single purpose or question. You can do this by listing all the different approaches that may be taken in your project through experimentation. Some of these might include:

1. Determining the effects that oil spills have on the growth of organisms.
2. Comparing health and disease statistics between different oil spill sites.
3. Determining the efficiency of a proposed solution such as bioremediation to neutralize and clean up oil from a spill.

After you have listed various approaches to your project, choose one that you think will produce a reasonable and practical experiment.

Given these choices, the first and second alternatives would probably be too broad to work with. Such experiments would require several years for you to compare the growth, health, and disease characteristics of several sites. The work would involve periodic studies of people, animals, and plants, in order to measure their overall health, function, endurance, immunity, and quality of vital functions. Although these are very challenging objectives that would make great long-term studies, they might be too much to satisfy your immediate objective within the time frame you have. However, the third alternative would be a great experiment because it focuses on a central idea, namely, it would study the efficiency of bioremediation (a natural means of using various microorganisms to consume fuel-derived toxins and turn them into carbon dioxide). You could measure the efficiency of various microorganisms in order to find out which one best eliminates oil in seawater. A procedural plan could easily be developed to parallel your purpose.

Step Two: Obtain Scientific Review Committee (SRC) Approval

Since many local, state, and regional science fairs are affiliated with the Intel ISEF, the format and instructions in this book are designed to help you create and present a science fair project that complies with Intel ISEF rules and guidelines. As such, it is important to provide a summary of Intel ISEF science project research and experimental guidelines that may affect your project. As soon as you have narrowed in on a project topic and defined your objective, you should consult with your science teacher or mentor about receiving Scientific Review Committee (SRC) approval before starting your project. Many local, state, and regional science fairs establish SRC approval deadlines long before the deadline for even entering your project in a science fair. Often this deadline is in November or December prior to the date of the science fair. The purpose of the SRC is to ensure the safety of the student performing the research and experiment as well as the subject being tested. The SRC also functions to disapprove research that may be inappropriate or illegal. Projects involving humans, vertebrate animals, pathogenic agents, or recombinant DNA must have SRC approval prior to the start of research.

Your science teacher or mentor is likely to be familiar with the rules and guidelines concerning SRC approval and probably has all the forms and paperwork you need in order to be in compliance. If not, contact your local, state, or

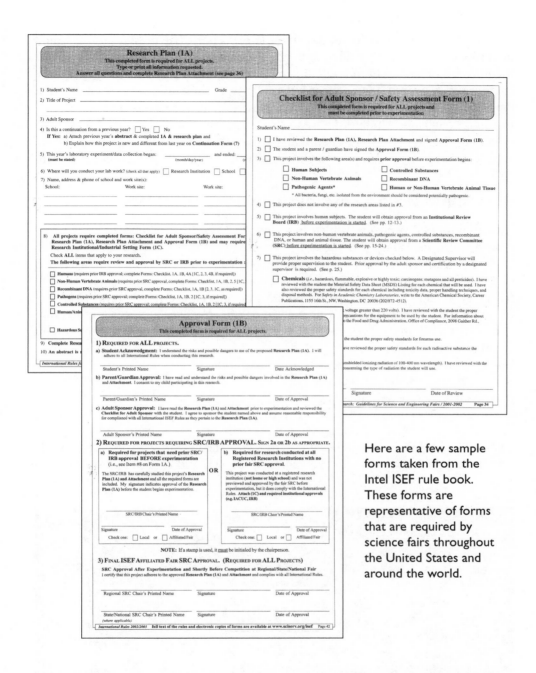

Here are a few sample forms taken from the Intel ISEF rule book. These forms are representative of forms that are required by science fairs throughout the United States and around the world.

regional science fair administrator to obtain SRC deadlines and the appropriate forms. For a complete listing of all current Intel ISEF–affiliated science fairs, please see Appendix D at the back of this book.

Step Three: Organize Your Experiment

One you have reduced your topic to a single purpose or question, you must organize your experiment. In the example regarding bioremediation of oil spills, you must organize an experiment that will allow you to measure the efficiency of various microorganisms in neutralizing the presence of oil in seawater. It would be difficult (not to mention illegal) to add home heating oil to a body of water for the purpose of testing bioremediation over a short time period, so a more practical thing to do would be to collect several large buckets of natural seawater that you can add home heating oil to along with your microorganism variables and test in an environmentally safe area. Your objective would then be to study the effects of various microorganisms in the bioremediation of home heating oil. After you have organized your experiment, you must develop a procedural plan.

Step Four: Create an Experimental Procedural Plan

An experimental procedural plan is a uniform, systematic approach to testing your hypothesis. When you begin this phase you should make a step-by-step list of what you will do to test your hypothesis. To start, first *correlate* (i.e., bring one thing into a reciprocal relationship with another) what you want to prove. You begin by selecting one thing to change in each experiment. Things that are changed are called *variables*. You want to be able to correlate two or more variables—the *dependent* variable and the *independent* variable. The dependent variable is the one that is being measured; the independent variable is the one that is controlled or manipulated by the experiment. For example, you may want to see whether the health and growth of a tomato plant (the dependent variable) is influenced by the amount of light the plant is exposed to (the independent variable). The correlation here is between the health of a plant and light exposure. Several other independent variables may be used instead, such as water, oxygen, carbon dioxide, nitrogen levels, and so on. However, for the sake of clarity we will use only light as a variable for this example. You should then state how you will

This student posed the question, "Does an Asphalt Road or a Concrete Sidewalk Create Less Friction than a Linoleum Floor" for his project topic. Here, the correlation was between surface type and amount of friction.

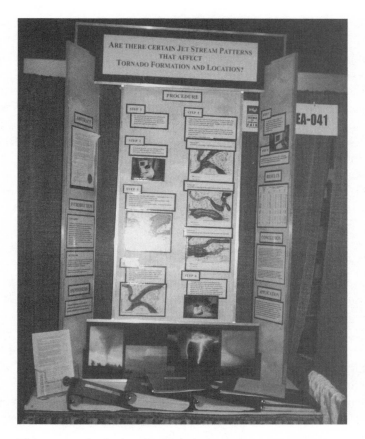

This project looked at the correlation between jet stream patterns and the formation and location of a tornado.

change your independent variable and how you will measure the amount of change in the dependent variable.

Establish a Control Group

Next, an experimental group and a control group must be established. The control group provides you with a basis for comparing the experimental group. For example, you may have an experimental group of tomato plants, which is placed in a sunny window for two weeks and watered periodically. At the end of the period, the plants have grown three inches and are very green. At this point, you may conclude that sunlight does indeed increase plant growth. But before you draw this conclusion, you should determine whether the tomato plants would have grown and become green without any sunlight at all. This is where a *control group* of plants is needed. A control group is used for purposes of comparison with the experimental group so that you can see what occurred by changing your variables.

The control group of plants in our example would be those plants that are given the same treatment as the experimental ones, with the exception that they would not be exposed to sunlight. If the outcome of the experiment were a significant difference between the two groups, then you probably would be justified in concluding that tomato plant growth is influenced by the amount of sunlight the plant receives.

The procedural plan in this example is very simple, but it gives you an idea of the process of an experiment. In essence, the procedural plan advances from one stage to another in an organized fashion. Remember, however, that most experiments are not as simple as the one described here. Often obstacles arise and other interesting characteristics of the subject are revealed in the process. You may even discover existing differences in several trials with only one variable. In fact, this is a frequent occurrence, and it is an important reason why you must keep accurate data records (see Chapter 5).

Step Five: Conduct Your Experiment

Once you have established your procedural plan for your experiment and have received approval, it is time to collect the materials you will need. You may also need to obtain approval or permission to work in a laboratory or other professional environment. The important thing to keep in mind as you put your procedural plan into action is to collect accurate data results from repeated trials with the same variables and record all of your data for later analysis (see Chapter 5 for this important next step). The benefit to taking this approach is that it increases the accuracy of your results and conclusions. How many times do you need to repeat your experimental procedural plan? This really depends on many different factors, not the least of which is your subject matter.

Note: Appendix C in the back of this book contains the listings of several science project supply companies that may be able to provide you with the supplies and equipment you need to carry out your experiment. However, if you have a mentor who is a professional scientist or engineer, you may already have the supplies and equipment you need through the mentor's affiliation with a university or company research laboratory.

Avoiding a Failed Experiment

There are several reasons why an experiment may fail to validate a hypothesis, prove a point, or simply do what it was intended to do, for example, mistakes in the way the experiment was carried out (procedural errors), a poor or incomplete final analysis, and an erroneous hypothesis.

Procedural Errors

To avoid procedural problems, you must be consistent and meticulous with your subject variables and controls over repeated trials. For example, in the experiment involving sunlight and tomato plants, if you gave the experimental group of tomato plants more water than the control group or planted them in a soil that contained more nitrogen, you would get artificial results. This means that you are failing to control or hold your variable constant. How can you determine whether it was the sunlight alone or in combination with other factors that made the experimental tomatoes flourish? The same problem with inconsistent maintenance of controls might apply if you were studying the behavior of your friends at a party for a psychological experiment. What would happen if you made your study obvious by taking notes or pictures? Your friends probably would be influenced by your behavior and would not act in their usual manner. In this case, as the old saying goes, "you cannot measure an experiment without affecting the result." These examples involve manipulated experiments that would yield useless data. Of course, other procedural problems may arise during an experiment, especially if poorly calibrated measuring instruments are used.

Poor Final Analysis

Even after a carefully controlled experiment is completed, errors can still occur, possibly resulting from an incorrect analysis of results. For example, if you concluded that a certain salve cures acne, on the basis of tests that were conducted on female adolescents but not male ones, your final analysis would be inconclusive. While the salve may have worked on the females you tested, it may not work on females in different age groups or on males of all age groups. Other problems with the final analysis may arise from mathematical errors or from data that are irrelevant to the topic.

Erroneous Hypothesis

When an experiment is completed, the results are sometimes quite different from those that were predicted. If this occurs, do not manipulate the results to fit the initial hypothesis. The hypothesis may have been incorrect or vague to begin with, and the experimental results were accurate. If such problems occur in your project, you can salvage your work by finding out why the results were different than expected or by explaining a new or unexpected observation or solution. This will show the judges that you understand the primary aspects that concern your project topic, including the control and handling of variables in experimentation, repeated trials, and approach to reaching conclusions. This actually happens to be a judging criterion that many students overlook. So, if your experimental results are different from what you expected after several trials, take advantage of this situation by thoroughly analyzing and knowing why you received the results you did. (For more information about the criteria judges look for when judging a science fair project, see Chapter 7.)

Keep in mind that many scientific investigations do not support their specific goals. However, this does not weaken the validity or value of these investigations. In fact, many experiments require repeated testing and exploration to understand a particular phenomenon. Sometimes, unexpected experimental results lead to surprising discoveries and more interesting science projects!

Summary

1. The experiment is an essential part of your science project. It should test, survey, compare, and ultimately aim to solve or answer the problem or question presented.

2. You must focus your topic on an experimental approach that will clearly test your hypothesis and will uphold the scientific method.

3. After you decide on an experimental approach, you must develop a way of testing your subject. This involves defining your objective, obtaining Scientific Review Committee approval, organizing your experiment, and creating an experimental procedural plan.

4. An experimental group containing variables and a control group must be established as part of the experimental procedural plan. Several trials should be made with the same variables to ensure consistent data results from which conclusions can be made.

5. Three common ways in which an experiment can fail are procedural errors, poor final analysis, and an erroneous hypothesis.

5

ORGANIZING AND PRESENTING DATA

A vital part of the scientific method is being able to analyze your results and observations (data) so that you can form a sound conclusion. This is basically performed through two means of analyses: qualitative analysis and quantitative analysis. Qualitative analysis is not based on measurements, rather it is a means of analysis that provides your observation; for example, "what components were found in a sample," or "whether an experimental group of plants performed better than the control group of plants." Quantitative analysis, on the other hand, is based purely on measurements and always involves numbers—for example, "how much of a given component is present in a sample," or "how much the experimental group of plants grew in comparison to the control group of plants." While qualitative analysis is important to the explanation of your results, it is quantitative analysis that truly expresses your ability as a student scientist to interpret your data in a more precise and objective way that will provide a useful means for the interpretation of your conclusions by others. The remainder of this chapter is devoted to the interpretation, use, and explanation of the numerical data you have gathered from your experiment.

A very important part of explaining your results and observations to others is by giving meaning to your numerical data and the conclusions you formed from it. Since you began your experiment, you have been gathering data. Data are essentially groups of figures for a given experiment. During the initial stages of an experiment, they may have little meaning so it is important that you compile and organize your data accurately for your final analysis, observations, and conclusions. A good way to keep data is to record them in your project journal. After you have written down all the experimental results in an organized way, you can easily refer to your results to make generalizations and conclusions. There are several methods of presenting data, including the basic tabular, graphic, and statistical methods.

Tabulating and Graphing

Raw data have little or no meaning in and of themselves. It is only when they are organized into tabular and graphic forms that they can be understood in terms of your project. The data results must be arranged so that a project observer or judge can quickly comprehend the results of the project at a glance. Tables are relatively simple to make and convey information with precision. Additionally, they form the basis for most graphs. The main points to consider are organization and coordination. For example, consider these recordings in tabular form of the body temperature of a flu patient:

Times	Body Temperature (°F)
6:00 A.M.	97.0
8:00 A.M.	98.0
10:00 A.M.	99.0
Noon	100.0
2:00 P.M.	101.0
4:00 P.M.	102.0
6:00 P.M.	103.0
8:00 P.M.	102.0
10:00 P.M.	100.0
Midnight	98.0

If you want to see how the patient's temperature fluctuated during the day, you can do this by analyzing the table. But if you wanted to see at a glance how the patient's temperature changed, a graphic representation would be more effective.

A line graph may be used for this analysis. A line graph is composed of two axes: the x, or horizontal, and the y, or vertical. The x axis contains all the points for one set of data, and the y axis contains all the points for the other set of data.

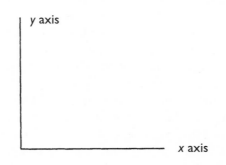

For example, you could label a range of body temperatures on the y axis and label the times on the x axis. After your axes are labeled, simply plot the points. Plotting involves matching each temperature with the corresponding time and marking them on the graph. For example, at 6:00 A.M. the body temperature was 97 degrees Fahrenheit, so you should locate and mark the point on the x and y axes at which 6:00 A.M. and 97 degrees correspond. Then do this for the rest of the data and connect the points to complete the graph.

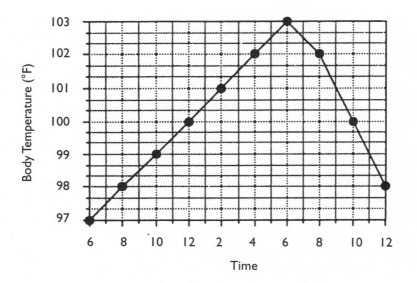

From this graph, we can quickly see that the patient's body temperature rose gradually, peaked late in the day, and fell during the evening.

Another means of graphical representation that makes data easy to understand is the pie chart. Suppose that you are testing a specimen of blood to determine the percentage of its composition of erythrocytes, leukocytes, and thrombocytes. After several tests and microscopical observation you conclude that the blood contained the percentages shown in the following table:

Cell Type	% Composition
Erythrocytes	50.0
Thrombocytes	38.0
Leukocytes	12.0
	$\Sigma^* = 100.00\%$

The data can be represented in a pie chart:

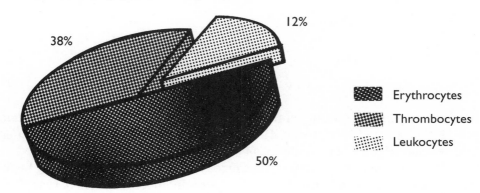

$^*\Sigma$ is a Greek symbol that means "the summation of."

Each section represents a percentage of the pie. It is easy to see that the leukocyte blood count is low in terms of its percentage of the total composition.

There are many other ways to graph your data besides the two methods shown. The important thing to remember about graphing is that it summarizes your results in a visual form that emphasizes the differences between groups of data results. As the old saying goes, a picture is worth a thousand words.

The Statistical Method

Some very simple statistics will allow you to expand on your data analysis. Some of these applications include: the *mean, frequency distribution,* and *percentile.*

The **mean,** expressed as $\bar{x}$, where x is any rational number, is a mathematical average that is really the central location of your data. The sum of your data numbers is denoted by the symbol Σ, which means "the summation of." This sum is then divided by the quantity of your data recordings, which is the symbol n. Thus the mean is expressed as this formula:

$$\bar{x} = \frac{\Sigma x}{n}$$

For example, consider the mean fluoride level in parts per million (ppm) from 11 different water departments.

Town Name	Fluoride Level (ppm)
A-Town	1.00
B-Town	1.50
C-Town	1.50
D-Town	0.05
E-Town	0.04
F-Town	1.01
G-Town	0.09
H-Town	0.05
I-Town	2.00
J-Town	1.00
K-Town	1.00
	$\Sigma(x) = 9.24$

Using the formula, you can express your results as follows: If $\Sigma(x) = 9.24$ and $n = 11$, then $\bar{x} = 9.24/11 = 0.8400$. The figure .8400 is the mean, or the mathematical average, of the studied water plants.

Now suppose that you collected samples from 50 water plants. It may be difficult to generalize about the results, so a better method is needed to record the data. One way of describing the results statistically is with a **frequency distribution.** This method is a summary of a set of observations showing the number of items in several categories. For example, suppose that the following levels were observed to be present in 50 samples:

Fluoride Levels (ppm)	Frequency (f)
2.0	3
1.70	6
1.50	7
1.00	8
0.90	10
0.80	7
0.50	6
0.04	3
	$\Sigma f = 50\,n$

These results can then be graphed using a histogram, which represents your frequency distribution. With a histogram, your item classes are placed along the horizontal axis and your frequencies along the vertical axis. Then rectangles are drawn with the item classes as the bases and frequencies as the sides. This type of diagram is useful because it clearly shows that the fluoride levels are normally at the 0.90 to 1.00 ppm mark (see diagram).

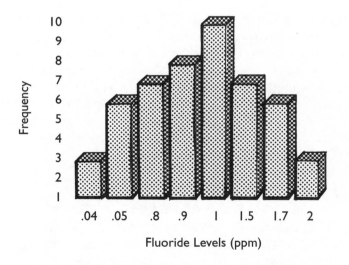

The **percentile** is another useful statistic. A percentile is the position of one value from a set of data that expresses the percentage of the other data that lie below this value. To calculate the position of a particular percentile, first put the values in ascending order. Then divide the percentile you want to find by 100 and multiply by the number of values in the data set. If the answer is not an integer (a positive or negative whole number), round up to the next position of the data value you're looking for. If the answer is an integer, average the data values of that position and the next higher one for the data value you're looking for. For example, suppose that you wanted to test the efficiency of 11 automobiles by measuring how many miles each car gets to a gallon of gasoline. You have recorded the following data: 17.6, 16.4, 18.6, 16.1, 16.3, 15.9, 18.9, 19.7, 19.1, 20.2, and 19.5. First, you would arrange the numbers in ascending order: 15.9, 16.1, 16.3, 16.4, 17.6, 18.6, 18.9, 19.1, 19.5, 19.7, and 20.2. Now suppose that you want to determine which car ranked in the 90th percentile. To calculate the 90th percentile for this data set, write this equation: $(90/100)(11) = 9.9$. Since 9.9 is not an integer, round up to 10, and the tenth value is your answer. The tenth value is 19.7; therefore, the car that traveled 19.7 miles per gallon of gasoline is in the 90th percentile, and 90 percent of the cars in your study were less gas efficient.

In summary, you will have to decide which technique works best for your type of data. You can usually express your results in terms of either standard mathematical or statistical graphing. However, there are occasions when only one type will work. If you are dealing with numerous figures or classes of figures, a statistical graph usually works best. For example, if you wanted to demonstrate the variation of test scores between boys and girls in the eighth grade, you would probably make your point clearer by using the statistical method, which would allow you to find the percentiles in which each student scored and the mean test score. On the other hand, if you were investigating the mineral composition of water, the best way to represent the proportion of its contents might be through a pie chart.

Other Means for Representing Data

Since every project is different you may find that you will need other means for showing and explaining your data results. For example, if you need to refer to various stages of a science project experiment that was conducted over a long period of time where measurements may have been taken at various stages at specific times, a **time line** might be a better means of representing your data (see the diagram below). Additionally, if you need to describe the results of a repeated process or a sequence and it is cumbersome to do so through text, a series of **flow charts** may be useful and may make your project data results visually interesting (see the example on the following page).

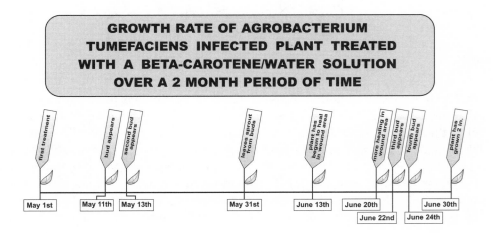

GROWTH RATE OF AGROBACTERIUM TUMEFACIENS INFECTED PLANT TREATED WITH A BETA-CAROTENE/WATER SOLUTION OVER A 2 MONTH PERIOD OF TIME

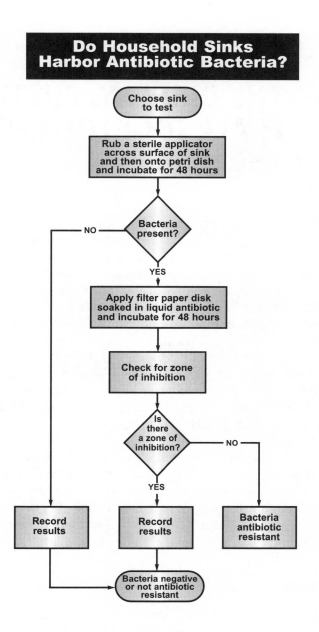

Do Household Sinks Harbor Antibiotic Bacteria?

Choose sink to test

Rub a sterile applicator across surface of sink and then onto petri dish and incubate for 48 hours

Bacteria present?

NO

YES

Apply filter paper disk soaked in liquid antibiotic and incubate for 48 hours

Check for zone of inhibition

Is there a zone of inhibition?

NO

YES

Record results

Record results

Bacteria antibiotic resistant

Bacteria negative or not antibiotic resistant

Summary

1. Data are groups of figures or results you recorded from conducting your experiment. They are organized for observation and drawing conclusions about your experiment.

2. The tabular, graphic, and statistical methods are some of the basic ways of calculating and presenting data.

3. Some basic ways to show your data so that others can see your results at a glance are through the use of line graphs, pie charts, bar graphs, time lines, and flow charts.

6

THE DISPLAY: PUTTING IT ALL TOGETHER FOR THE FAIR

The display is an essential part of your project. Although it alone will not save a bad project, it can enhance the success of a good one. There is nothing more disappointing than to have a judge or viewer overlook a meritorious project purely on the basis of its illegible or disorganized display. Therefore, it is worth spending some extra time making an attractive display.

Due to the guidelines established by the Intel ISEF, most state and regional fairs have put the emphasis on a "poster session" approach, where the backboard is the focal point of the display accompanied by a report and abstract. In general, your display should consist of a great-looking backboard and report both containing text, tables, graphs, charts, photographs, and diagrams to fully illustrate and explain your project.

Your exhibit should show all aspects of your project. There are many ways to do this, but you must remember that all information on the backboard should be clearly and concisely summarized to allow the viewer to grasp the essence of the project quickly. Lengthy discussions should be confined to the report. Only certain items from your project can be displayed. See "Display Restrictions" in this chapter for a general list of what can and cannot be displayed at the science fair.

The Backboard

The backboard is usually the most important part of your display. It should include all the major parts of your project. The backboard is essentially an upright, self-supporting board with organized highlights of your project. It is usually three-sided, although it does not necessarily have to be. The backboard should meet the spacing standards of the Intel ISEF if you plan to enter your project in a state or regional fair that is affiliated with the ISEF. The dimensions of your display must not be more than 108 inches (274 centimeters) high, including the table; 30 inches (76 centimeters) deep, and 48 inches (122 centimeters) wide. If these dimensions are exceeded, you may be disqualified.

When constructing your backboard, stay away from thin posterboard or cardboard. Backboards made of these materials will bend and do not look very professional. Instead, purchase a firm, self-supporting material such as a reinforced paperboard or corkboard. In the long run, you will find these types of

The Use of Yeast Artificial Chromosomes to Mimic the Natural Setting of the Human β—Globin Locus

BI-054

BI-056

Most state and regional fairs have put emphasis on a "poster session" approach where the backboard is the focal point of the display.

materials easier to work with and more attractive. Alternatively, you may choose to purchase a premade backboard. In recent years this has become a popular choice among students. Two companies that specialize in the sale of premade backboards are *Showboard* and *Science Fair Supply.* Both offer backboards in a variety of sizes and materials and even offer other project display accessories. You can reach Showboard at 1-800-323-9189 or visit their Web site: www.showboard.com. Science Fair Supply can be reached at 1-800-556-3247 or online at: www.sciencefairsupply.com.

Select appropriate lettering for your backboard. Use your computer's word processor or purchase graphic design software that allows you to make a neat, attractive presentation on your backboard. If you do not have software that will allow you to do this, you might want to purchase self-sticking letters or make use of the services of a professional printer. In recent years, almost all science fair project backboards (at the state and international level) have typeface styles and background patterns that have been rendered in one of many terrific graphic design software programs. If you do not have such a program on your home computer, your school probably has one. Whichever program you choose, keep in mind that because so many options are available, it is simply unacceptable to handprint your backboard especially if you are aiming for a top-notch project.

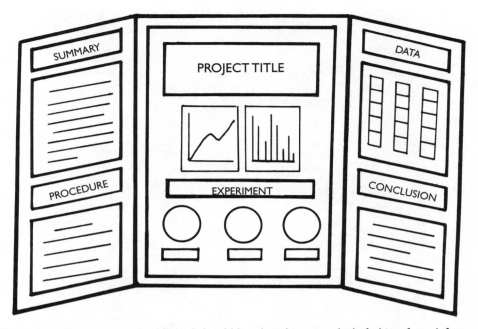

The information on your backboard should be placed in an orderly fashion from left to right under organized headings.

Now that you know how to construct a backboard, you need to know what information you should put on it and where to place it. There is no standard way of making a backboard; however, all the information displayed on it should be well organized. The project title, for example, should stand out in the middle section in bold print. The rest of your information should be placed in an orderly fashion from left to right under organized headings that follow the scientific method. You can also apply headings that relate more specifically to your subject. Whatever headings you choose, make sure they are explicit so that a viewer can grasp each element of your project quickly and efficiently.

The information that you place under each heading is crucial. It must be concise and inclusive. Do not fill up your backboard with excess information. Try to summarize the facts under each heading in no more than 300 words. Additional backboard space can be filled with additional visual information on your subject.

The Report

It is also important that your report be of good quality. This means that you must organize a portfolio of clearly stated, factual information. It is important to keep this in mind because the report is essentially your spokesperson when you are not with your project (for example, during preliminary judging).

An organized report contains the historical background on your subject, an introduction that states your purpose, a procedure that explains your means of acquiring information, your plan for organizing an experiment, and all the recorded data, diagrams, flow charts, photos, conclusions, and other details that fully explain

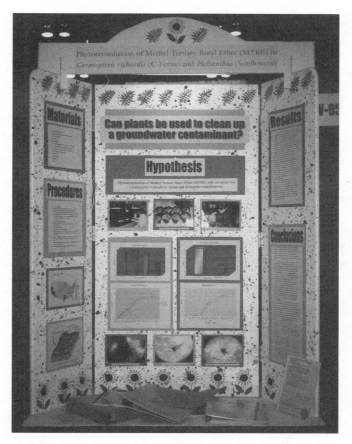

Your backboard should be neat and contain pertinent information laid out in an orderly fashion from left to right under organized headings, including graphs and photographs.

your project. You might even want to include detailed descriptions about different phases in your experiment in the form of a diary. It is a good idea to include the names and places you have visited, together with any related correspondence.

Your report may be easier to complete if you create a journal when you begin to work on your project. If you record everything in your journal as you go along, all you will need to do later is organize your notes, since your journal is essentially the foundation of your report.

In organizing your report, you will have to distinguish between primary and secondary sources of information. Primary sources of information consist of surveys, observations, and experimentation that you have done either alone or through a mentor. Secondary sources are outside sources, such as the library, media organizations, government agencies, companies, laboratories, and so on. If you have used secondary sources for information either quoted directly or used indirectly, you must acknowledge these sources in footnotes and in a bibliography. Also, if you have worked under the guidance of a mentor or adviser be sure to give credit to this person and those who have assisted you in a references section in the report.

As with your backboard, make sure you prepare the report with word processing software on your computer. Never handprint the report. A report will not be able to explain your project as well as you can, but it is reassuring to know that an organized report can work well for you in your absence.

If you write a thorough report that encompasses all of the items mentioned here, you may be eligible to submit it to another type of science competition, such as the Intel Science Talent Search, a local Junior Science and Humanities Symposium, or another similar competition. For more information on these types of science competitions, see Appendix E.

The Abstract

An abstract is a brief summary of your project that is 250–300 words long. The abstract briefly explains the project's purpose and procedural plan and presents generalized data and a short discussion of your conclusions. There is no standard way to write an abstract, but it should always be concise and clear. Many state and regional fairs have made the abstract a mandatory part of science fair project competition and specify that it must be completed and submitted to the science fair's Scientific Review Committee with an application for admission to the science fair. Many science fairs review the abstract to make sure that the project you

Abstract

Is Synthetic Motor Oil Spillage Environmentally Safer than Petroleum Motor Oil Spillage?

The impact of oil spillage is a great concern for the environment whether it be due to its regulated disposal or by accident. The purpose of this project is to determine, in the event of spillage, which form of motor oil, namely, regular petroleum motor oil or synthetic motor oil, would have the least negative impact on the environment. It was hypothesized that the regular petroleum motor oil would have the least negative impact since the synthetic motor oil contains man-made polymers. In order to test this theory, the growth rate of bean plants grown in soil containing traces of unused synthetic motor oil that was administered in various amounts and the growth rate of bean plants grown in the same soil containing traces of unused regular petroleum motor oil that was administered in the same amounts were compared against bean plants that were grown in the same soil where no traces of either type of oil were administered. The results indicated that every bean plant exposed to traces of oil was negatively impacted compared to the control group of bean plants. However, between the two types of oils studied herein, it was evident that the synthetic oil had more of a negative impact upon the plants as evidenced by retarded root length and the ability of the plants to sprout beans which were measured and recorded at various intervals and at the conclusion of the experiment. Therefore, my hypothesis was correct, the spillage of regular petroleum motor oil appears to have the least negative impact.

have been working on meets the standards proscribed by the fair's Scientific Review committee and the rules and regulations established by that science fair. The abstract further helps to categorize your project into the correct scientific category of competition, and it helps the judges to quickly grasp the summary of your project. It may even suggest to the judges that they should consider your work for other awards that are sponsored by outside special awards presenters.

The previous page contains a simple abstract of a recent award-winning science fair project to give you an idea of how an abstract is written.

Display Restrictions

You read in Chapter 3 about the project limitation guidelines established by the Intel ISEF. The Intel ISEF also has strict regulations involving the exhibition of certain articles in conjunction with the rest of your exhibit. The following is a

Safety restrictions may prevent you from displaying certain items. The best way to uphold these regulations and explain your project is through the use of photographs, drawings, and charts.

summary of the Intel ISEF display and safety rules. If you have any questions, contact your science fair administrator or Science Service, the organization that administers the Intel ISEF, for more information about what is acceptable for display.

A rule of thumb is to avoid anything that could be potentially hazardous to display in public. The intent of the rule is to protect other students and the public. You can usually uphold such regulations by using photographs, drawings, graphs, charts, and model simulations (where permissible) to show the results of your investigation and research.

If you have any doubts about displaying any part of your project, be sure to first check with officials from your local science fair or contact the Intel ISEF. The following is a summary of items that cannot be displayed.

Items That Cannot Be Displayed

1. Live animals, living organisms, preserved vertebrate/invertebrate animals, taxidermy specimens, or parts including embryos
2. All live materials, including plants and microbes
3. Human or animal parts or body fluids (i.e., blood or urine) except teeth, hair, nails, histological dry mount sections, and wet mount tissue slides properly acquired
4. All soil and waste samples and related materials
5. All chemicals including water and their containers
6. Poisons, drugs, controlled substances, or hazardous substances or devices (e.g., firearms, weapons, ammunition)
7. Food, human or animal
8. Syringes, pipettes, and similar devices and sharp objects
9. Dry ice or other sublimating solids (e.g., solids that can vaporize into a gas without first becoming a liquid)
10. Any flame, open or concealed
11. Highly flammable display materials
12. Tanks that have contained combustible gases or liquids, unless purged with carbon dioxide
13. Batteries with open top cells
14. Photographs and other visual presentations of surgical techniques, dissection, necropsies, and/or laboratory techniques depicting vertebrate animals in other-than-normal conditions
15. Operation of a Class III or IV laser

The following is a summary of items that can be displayed with certain restrictions:

Items That Can Be Displayed with Restrictions

(Check with your local science fair officials to determine how you can make these items suitable for display.)

1. Projects with unshielded belts, pulleys, chains and moving parts with tension or pinch points

2. Any device requiring voltage over 110 volts

3. Soil or waste samples if permanently encased

4. Empty tanks that previously contained combustible liquids or gases must be certified as having been purged with carbon dioxide

5. Class III and Class IV lasers (but may not be operated)

6. Class II lasers containing a sign that reads "Laser Radiation Do Not Stare into Beam," with a protective housing that prevents access to the beam, operated only during display, safety inspection, and judging

7. Large vacuum tubes or dangerous ray–generating devices must be properly shielded

8. Pressurized tanks that contained noncombustibles may be allowed if properly secured

9. Any apparatus producing temperatures that will cause physical burns must be adequately shielded

Summary

1. Your science project display is very important and should be presented in an organized and attractive manner.

2. The display should consist of a backboard containing summary information about your project under organized headings that are based on the scientific method, tables, graphs, charts, photographs and diagrams, a report, and an abstract.

3. Backboards must meet the standard space requirements established by the Intel ISEF, which are 108 inches (274 centimeters) high including table, 30 inches (76 centimeters) deep, and 48 inches (122 centimeters) wide.

4. The report can be created primarily from your project journal. It contains all the details about each step in your project along with flow charts and photographs that may be too cumbersome or inappropriate to display on your backboard.

5. An abstract is a short essay that summarizes the goals, methods, and conclusions of your project.

6. The Intel ISEF has established regulations for the restriction and modification of potentially hazardous items for display.

7

AT THE FAIR

This chapter will prepare you for what lies ahead. If you follow the format for completing a project that is recommended in this book, you should be successful. Make sure you have filled out all necessary forms and paperwork and are properly registered as a contestant at your state or regional science fair. This also involves getting your project listed in the correct category of competition.

There are basically two broad categories under which the majority of science fair projects can be categorized—**biological sciences** and **physical sciences.** There are many disciplines within each of these categories, and all of them are further distinguished at most science fairs by grade and by individual entrants or team entrants. The Intel ISEF breaks these categories down into the following scientific disciplines: the biological sciences category consists of projects that pertain to the life sciences—*behavioral and social sciences, biochemistry, botany, gerontology, medicine and health, microbiology,* and *zoology.*

The physical sciences category consists of projects that pertain to *chemistry, computer science, earth and space science, engineering, environmental science, mathematics,* and *physics.*

It is usually easy to determine the category where your project belongs, but sometimes it may be difficult. For example, if you did a project on human prosthetic limbs and joints, in which you studied the physics of how artificial joints wear after a period of time, in what category would your project belong? Well, if your project emphasized the amount of friction in a joint, it would probably be a physical sciences project. But if you began to discuss the biodegradability of the device, your project might be more appropriately placed in the biological sciences category. The wrong choice could hurt your outcome in the competition.

Setting Up Your Project

As you set up your project, pay careful attention to the space requirements mentioned in Chapter 6 (the space should be marked off). Your backboard and display should be self-supporting, but it is wise to bring spray mount, a stapler, glue, tape, and an extension cord (if applicable to your display) in case your project needs minor repairs or modifications.

After your project is completely set up, a fair representative will check it to make sure everything complies with the fair rules and safety regulations. Make sure that you have everything displayed properly and have any necessary instructions available for the fair staff or judges (this is especially important if you have a project that involves the use of a computer or some other type of mechanically operated display).

Judging at the State and Regional Fair

At some fairs, judging takes place as soon as all the projects are set up. Students and parents are not allowed in the exhibit hall during this time. Generally, judges are assigned to separate divisions as teams. They begin by reviewing the projects in their category individually and then as a group, in which they exchange thoughts with team members and rank the projects. While judging systems vary from science fair to science fair, typically, most state and regional fairs will spend one day on this type of preliminary judging in which they determine those projects that rank in the top 25–50%. These projects then qualify to compete for the second round of judging which is referred to as final judging. This final round determines place awards and eligibility of the best projects in grades 9–12 for the Intel ISEF.

During the final round of judging, state and regional science fair contestants who have made the first round cut (finalists) are invited to give an oral presentation for a variety of judges. The judges may represent the fair itself, professional and academic associations, or business that distribute specialized awards.

Most state and regional science fair judges score contestants on various criteria, including:

1. *Scientific approach to the problem/engineering goals.* This is often the most important and substantial criterion that is judged. This criterion measures whether the exhibitor shows evidence of applied scientific skill or engineering development through recognizing the scope and limitation of the issue that is being studied and addressing the scope of the problem including the quality of the work, time spent securing data, and whether the exhibitor's observations support this data.

2. *Creative ability/originality.* This criterion also weighs substantially in the exhibitor's score and basically measures the ingenuity and originality of the problem that is being studied and/or in the exhibitor's approach to the problem. Judges look for whether you have chosen the best method possible in your investigation and whether you have made the most effective use of materials, equipment, and techniques pertaining to your topic. They also take into account whether your project is unique, how you derived your topic, and credit you give to mentors who may have assisted you.

3. *Thoroughness and accuracy.* This area measures the depth of the literature used concerning the project as well as the quality of the experimental investigation and your use and analysis of data results.

4. *Clarity.* This criterion determines whether the project's scope, purpose, or goals are clear and concise. Exhibitors sometimes get swept away by the

At most science and regional fairs, contestants are asked to give several presentations for both fair and special award judges from different organizations and businesses.

complexity of their subject and fail to communicate their project's purpose to the judges. While it is admirable to acquire a new scientific or technical lingo while pursuing your topic, you will not impress anyone if you fail to communicate the topic clearly and concisely.

5. *Advancement of exhibitor's knowledge in science.* This area looks at whether the student has a good handle and understanding of the primary aspects that concern his or her topic, which includes both basic research and experimental principles.

6. *Other.* Some science fairs also grade your exhibit partly on its dramatic value—i.e., whether it is presented in a way that has visual appeal through the use of graphics, and workmanship. To the extent that you may be working with a partner on a team science fair project, an additional part of your overall score may include points on how the project was handled by the team, management, delegation and sharing of workload, expertise of each team member, and so on.

Keep in mind that judging is a difficult task that requires the skill and expertise of a wide range of qualified professionals. The judges are analyzing the overall quality of work that has been done on a subject matter that involves probing, testing, and reasoning in a creative sense. They are not interested in plain library research resembling a book report, meaningless collections, or copied work from books or other science fair projects that have been completed in previous years.

Presenting Your Project in an Interview

If you become a finalist, you will have the opportunity to be present with your project during judging, which is an enviable position. You will be able to explain in detail the research, procedures, methods, and conclusions in your project. Practice what you are going to say before the fair, so that your presentation will be smooth and relaxed. If possible, have your mentor, teacher, or someone familiar with your project interview you by asking you key questions that will likely be asked during judging.

Above all, the key is to be so well versed on your subject matter that you can handle any random questions that come your way. Judges want to see that you understand your project thoroughly and that you actually did the work yourself. They do not want to hear a memorized presentation that sounds like you are reciting a script. They want to be able to interject and ask you questions so they can see that you are thinking on your feet. They want to understand exactly what it is that you did and what you accomplished. If you cannot get these points across to a judge, you are not going to fare well, even if you conducted the most sophisticated experiment on the most interesting topic and achieved the most amazing results. None of this will matter if you do not communicate well to the judges. By being prepared to properly handle any question that might come your way, you will score very well with the judges.

The following is a list of the main questions you should be prepared to answer when you are presenting your project to a judge.

The Main Questions You Need to Be Able to Answer about Your Project

1. What is your project about?
2. Why did you select this project?
3. What did you expect to accomplish with your project?
4. Why did you choose the experiment that you did and did it provide the answers to what you were seeking?
5. What was your experimental plan, how did you gather your data, and can you explain the data you obtained? (Be prepared to use your display as a visual aid.)
6. Was this the best experiment to achieve your goal?
7. What conclusions have you drawn from this project, and what might be done to further your investigation in this project?

Remember, every now and then a judge will ask a question that no one could have anticipated and you may not have the answer for. If this happens to you, do not panic. Sometimes judges test you to see if you really did the work yourself and if you really have a handle on the subject matter of your project. While you should be able to answer anything about your project that you have on your backboard and in your report or abstract, you might be surprised by this type of trick question. If you find yourself in this situation, just explain to the judge that because your project covered so many different aspects of the topic you do not recall at the present time the answer to that particular question. You can also state that while you do not have the answer, you will certainly look into the question that was raised. Alternately, offer the judge an explanation on something related to this line of questioning that you might be familiar with (if you can do so), or just state that you are not familiar with the issue he or she is referring to but that you would be glad to inform the judge about another aspect concerning the project that is extremely relevant to the results you achieved.

It is important to realize that science fair judges at the state and regional level are typically experienced scientific researchers, engineers, mathematicians, doctors, and professors and are quite capable of detecting any errors or "fake" experimental results. They will also be able to tell if you just memorized your presentation or whether someone else did the work for you and if you do not have a working knowledge of your subject. Those individuals were selected as judges because they have a high level of expertise in a particular scientific discipline, which may incidentally be the category in which your project is entered at the fair. Also, be aware that the judge may have already seen a project similar to yours at another science fair.

Judging usually takes from a few hours to a full day with breakout sessions for lunch and workshops. Try to be consistent with every judge interviewing you; stay alert, and concentrate on what you want to say even though you may have already said the same thing to the last judge. If you must leave your project momentarily, leave a note stating that you will return soon. General tips to keep in mind for a successful presentation are: know your material, be thorough, be confident, communicate well, and enjoy a wonderful experience!

And the Winner Is . . .

After final judging, scores are tallied and the winners in each division are announced. The top high school projects of an Intel ISEF–affiliated state or regional fair qualify for competition in the Intel ISEF. Simply making it to the state or regional fair is an honor, but only a few can experience the prestige of participating in the Intel ISEF. Please see Chapter 1 for more information about this competition and Appendix E about alternative science fair project competitions.

Specialized Awards

Some science fairs include special areas of competition that are separate from the general fair honors. These special categories are accessible to students who complete a project concentrated in a particular area of science. Various companies and organizations present special awards. These groups honor excellence in a subject area related to the particular field that their organization specializes in, and these awards sometimes consist of prestigious scholarships, grants, and internships.

Closing Notes

This book was written to alleviate the frustration that often arises when students begin a science fair project. It attempts to explain the strategies and secrets often used by top winners. Although this book cannot guarantee that you will make it to the top with your science fair project, it can improve your chances and increase your motivation for future successes. Chances are good that your achievement will be recognized by college and business recruiters who are looking for science talent and dedication. Remember, many of today's respected scientists, engineers, doctors, and college professors began their careers by participating in science fairs. You, too, can follow in their footsteps by investing your time and talent in a science fair project.

Summary

1. It is important to check with your teacher or science fair officials to register your project properly and on time in the correct science fair category and division.

2. There are two broad categories under which the majority of science fair projects can be categorized—**biological sciences** and **physical sciences.** There are many disciplines within each category and all of them are further distinguished at most science fairs by grade and by individual entrants or team entrants.

3. While judging systems vary from science fair to science fair, most state and regional fairs typically spend one day on preliminary judging where those projects that rank in the top 25–50 percent are determined. These projects qualify to compete for the second round of judging, which is referred to as final judging.

4. Most state and regional science fair judges score contestants on these five basic criteria:
    a. Scientific approach to the problem/engineering goals
    b. Creative ability/originality
    c. Thoroughness and accuracy
    d. Clarity
    e. Advancement of the exhibitor's knowledge in science

5. In order to do well presenting your project to a judge, try to be so well-versed on your subject matter that you can handle any random questions that come your way.

II

50 Award-Winning Science Fair Projects

Important Notes before You Begin

The following pages contain outline samples for 50 award-winning science fair projects. The summaries and diagrams should help to advise you on how to prepare your project, particularly if you are a first-time science fair participant. These outlines are not intended to do the work for you but to provide you with a variety of useful models to follow. The results of these 50 projects have thus been eliminated, and lists of questions have been prepared instead, so that you may have a guide for drawing conclusions about the projects.

The summaries of five International Science and Engineering Fair projects are marked and included throughout in order to give you a sense of the caliber that is required for this highest level of competition. You will see that one of the ISEF projects appears again in a different form (see projects 37 and 38). This second experiment is included so you can see how successful science fair projects can be further researched and developed into even more successful projects.

As you read through these projects, you may require information about where to obtain some of the scientific equipment mentioned in the experiments. Refer to Appendix C for a list of scientific supply companies from which laboratory equipment and other supplies may be purchased in your area. Also, some experiments list metric units of measure that may be unfamiliar to you or may require conversion to conventional units of measure. Refer to the metric conversion table at the beginning of the book for information about converting measurements.

Finally, you should keep in mind that the project outlines come from a variety of scientific disciplines and require minimal to advanced levels of scientific skill. They were developed by actual students in grades 7 through 12 and do not come from a lab workbook. Thus, there is no guarantee that any of the experimental procedures for any project will work as the experiment may indicate. The outlines represent award-winning work from different grade levels. Therefore, while students with little scientific experience may find some of the projects difficult, they should find others particularly suitable. Where noted, the assistance of a research scientist is required or precautions must be taken, and special skills are needed for certain projects. Be sure to heed these notices if you sample these projects. They are there for your safety and to let you know whether or not a particular project is for you. In addition, check with your science fair project advisor for further guidance and safety precautions before starting any project appearing in this book. Most important, exercise common sense and good judgment when conducting any science experiment.

1

Which Characteristic Is Most Influential in Attracting Bees to a Flower: Fragrance, Color, or Flavor?

Note: Protective clothing should be worn and caution exercised when approaching the beehive.

Purpose

To determine the fragrance, color, and flavor that are most attractive to bees. Then, to determine which of these three characteristics plays the most important role in attracting bees.

Materials Needed

- pencil
- ruler
- 6 pieces of poster board
- 9 assorted types of flowers
- scissors
- food processor
- cheesecloth
- cup
- brush
- colored construction paper (9 different shades are necessary: white, red, orange, yellow, green, blue, violet, light pink, and hot pink)
- glue
- sugar, lemon juice, salt, and chokecherries (or a food with a similarly bitter taste)
- beehive
- protective clothing

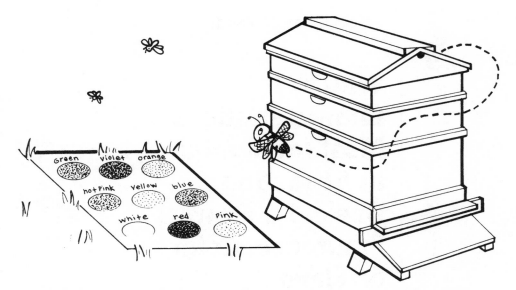

First, each poster board will be placed in front of the beehive to see which specific fragrance, color, and flavor are most attractive to the bees. Then, the three posters containing the separated variables only will be placed side by side to see which characteristic is most influential.

Experiment

The fragrance, color, and flavor variables will be isolated to identify the one that bees tend to go to first. For the fragrance test, several flowers that bees are known to pollinate will be pulverized individually in a food processor and strained through cheesecloth to collect the residue. The residue will then be streaked into separate circles on a poster board. For the color test, circles will be cut out of nine different shades of paper and glued onto another piece of poster board. For the flavor test, various flavors will be smeared over another poster board surface. Then, combinations of the three variables will be made. The bees' reactions and selections will be recorded.

Procedure

1. Draw nine 5-inch (12.7-cm) -diameter circles on one of the poster boards. Be sure to space them evenly on the board.

2. Obtain nine types of flowers and cut them from their stems. Pulverize them individually in a food processor. Then strain each pulverized flower through cheesecloth into the cup. With a brush, spread the residue from each flower in a separate circle on the poster board. Be sure to label the type of flower each smear came from.

3. Cut a 5-inch (12.7-cm) -diameter circle out of each sheet of construction paper. Space them randomly and evenly on another piece of poster board and glue them in place.

4. Take samples of the four basic food tastes (sweet, sour, salty, and bitter) from the sugar, lemon juice, salt, and chokecherries, and spread them separately on the third poster board. Be sure to label them.

5. For the remaining three poster boards, create the following combinations of characteristics: place each flower fragrance on a separate colored circle, place each flavor on a separate colored circle, and finally, mix the flavors with the various flower fragrances. Be sure to label them.

6. Begin your experiment with the first poster board of fragrances. Place the board approximately six feet (two meters) in front of the beehive and stand several feet further away. Note the fragrance to which the bees are consistently attracted. Remove the board and replace it with the board that contains only colors. Again, stand several feet away and see what color most attracts the bees. Do the same with the flavor board to see which flavor the bees are drawn to. Record your observations.

7. Verify your results by trying the combination boards. For example, if the bees in step 6 favored the color violet, a sweet flavor, and the fragrance of lilacs, see if those results hold true when the violet circle is covered with either the sugar or lilac residue.

8. Test to see which of the three characteristics is the most influential in attracting the bees by placing all three poster boards from step 6 side by side in front of the hive. Note the board that most consistently attracts the bees.

Results

1. Were all the bees consistent in their preferences?

2. What fragrance, color, and flavor seemed to most attract the bees?

3. Did the bees tend to favor the same fragrance when it was combined with different colors and flavors? Did the same hold true for the color and flavor variables?

4. Which single characteristic appeared to be the most influential in attracting bees?

2

The Effects of Gender Identity on Short-Term Memory

Purpose

To graph and compare the effects of gender identity on the short-term memories of varying age groups of children.

Materials Needed

- 50 human subjects:
  5 boys and 5 girls in 1st grade
  5 boys and 5 girls in 2nd grade
  5 boys and 5 girls in 3rd grade
  5 boys and 5 girls in 4th grade
  5 boys and 5 girls in 5th grade

- grid containing 20 simple black and white pictures traditionally gender-typed for males (for example, a football) and for females (for example, a doll), arranged in alternate positions.

- stopwatch

Experiment

Each subject will be given 15 seconds to study the grid pictures. When the grid is taken away, the subject will be asked to list the names of the objects he or she can recall. It is believed that children will recall objects traditionally associated with their own gender.

Procedure

1. Test a child from each grade group individually in a quiet room that is free of distractions. Read the following directions to the participants: "I will show you some pictures for 15 seconds. When the time is up, I will take the pictures away and ask you to list the names of as many pictures as you can remember."

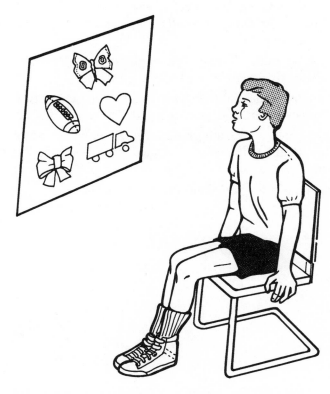

Each child will be given 15 seconds to study traditionally gender-typed grid pictures. When the grid is taken away, the subject will be asked to list the names of the objects he or she can recall.

2. Tabulate the results using two different methods of analysis.

   First Analysis: Group your data according to whether each subject remembers a majority or a minority of the items traditionally associated with his or her gender or simply an equal number of both male- and female-gender-typed pictures.

   Second Analysis: Examine whether there is a tendency for each age group, as well as the group as a whole, to be influenced by the gender-typing of the pictures presented. Record the total number and percentage of the male-gender-typed pictures recalled by the subjects as a group, and do the same with the female-gender-typed pictures. Do this for each grade level.

Results

1. Did the boys, as a whole group, recall a majority or a minority of male-gender-typed pictures? Or, did they recall an equal number of male- and female-gender-typed pictures?

2. Did the girls, as a whole group, recall a majority or a minority of female-gender-typed pictures? Or, did they recall an equal number of male- and female-gender-typed pictures?

3. When grouped by grade, did the boys recall male-gender-typed pictures at a greater frequency than female-gender-typed pictures?

4. When grouped by grade, did the girls recall female-gender-typed pictures at a greater frequency than male-gender-typed pictures?

5. Do the results change for each grade level? If so, what variables may have influenced the results of the varying grade levels? What are the implications of these results?

6. What do your results tell you about the group as a whole?

3

Do All Plants Transpire at the Same Rate under Different Sources of Light?

Purpose

To determine if various species of plants transpire at the same rate under different sources of light.

Materials Needed

- 12 2-liter plastic soda bottles
- potting soil (enough to fill 12 soda bottle bottoms)
- scissors or cutting tool
- 3 young specimens each of 4 plant species (suggested: jade plant, African violet, ivy, polka dot plant)
- 3 cups (0.6 liter) water
- fluorescent lamp
- household lamp
- sunlight
- spatula
- graduated measuring cup

Experiment

Three plants of four different species will be placed in the removable bottoms of 12 plastic soda bottles. The removable tops of the soda bottles will be cut to fit within the soda bottle bottoms to form a kind of convertible terrarium. One sample of each plant species will be placed in the presence of all three different light sources: direct sunlight, a fluorescent lamp, and a household lamp, for a period of 6 hours. The amount of transpiration of the plants will then be compared and recorded.

Procedure

1. Pull the plastic supporting bottoms from the soda bottles and fill them with potting soil. Then cut the rounded bases from the upper portions of the soda bottles and put them aside.

2. Transplant the plants into the soda bottle bottoms.

3. Water each plant with ¼ cup (0.05 liter) of water and fit the soda bottle tops over the plants to create a terrarium (this will allow you to trap and measure the amount of water that the plants transpire). Be sure to place labels on each bottle top to specify the type of plant and the light source to which it will be exposed.

4. Place each plant species in the presence of all three light sources for 6 hours.

5. After the light exposure, remove the upper portions of the soda bottles carefully so that the water that has transpired onto them will not roll off. Then remove the water from each container with a spatula and measure with the measuring cup the quantity of water that transpired from each plant.

6. Repeat Steps 4 and 5 several times to obtain more accurate results.

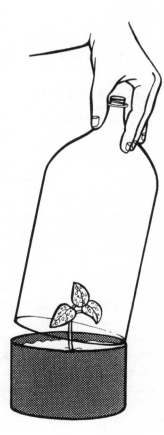

The plastic supporting bottoms will be removed from 2-liter soda bottles and used as pots for the various plants. Then, the rounded bases of the upper portions of the soda bottles will be cut to fit over the plants to form a terrarium.

Results

1. What amounts of water did each plant transpire under the different light sources?

2. Did the same plant species transpire equal amounts of water under all three light sources?

3. Which light source induced the most transpiration?

4. What outside variables may have influenced your results?

4

Can Plant Cloning Be Used Effectively by Produce Growers?

Purpose

To try to make a more perfect carrot and green bean by cloning rather than using the traditional cultivating methods, which may yield a lesser-quality vegetable or one that contains artificial chemicals and sprays. Also, to determine whether cloning is a faster and more effective means for farmers to grow crops.

Materials Needed

- carrot seeds from an unblemished organically grown carrot
- green bean seeds (same as above)
- pots for plants
- vermiculite
- greenhouse incubator
- seed germination medium
- glass beaker
- bunsen burner

- 30 petri dishes
- potting soil
- scalpel and forceps
- 5 fluid ounces (150 ml) callus initiation medium
- plastic bags
- 5 fluid ounces (150 ml) clone induction medium

Experiment

Some of the carrot and green bean seeds will be planted in vermiculite (to serve as a control of a traditional cultivating method) and some in the seed germination medium that has been melted into some of the petri dishes. After this latter group has grown, they will be transferred to the callus initiation medium then to the clone induction medium. The growth rates of the plants and the quality of their produce will be analyzed in comparison to the control plants and produce.

Procedure

1. Plant some of the carrot and green bean seeds in pots of vermiculite and put them into the greenhouse incubator. These will serve as the control group.

2. Melt the seed germination medium in the glass beaker over the bunsen burner and pour it into ten petri dishes equally. When solid, drop some of the carrot and green bean seeds onto the surface of the petri dishes. Growth will show in two weeks. These will serve as the experimental group.

3. When the plants in the control group are at least 4 inches (11.5 cm) tall, uproot them and put them into pots of potting soil. When the experimental plants are also 4 inches (11.5 cm) tall, cut their roots and leaves off with the scalpel. Cut their remaining stems into ½-inch (1-cm) pieces. Melt the callus initiation medium in the beaker over the bunsen burner and pour equally into ten other petri dishes. Next, place the stem sections onto the solidified petri dishes. Cover the dishes and put them into plastic bags.

4. Within a month, shoots will be visible. At this time, melt the clone induction medium and pour it into the remaining ten petri dishes. Using the scalpel, cut around the stem sections, including the callus initiation medium. With forceps, place the cuttings on the solidified clone induction medium. Cover the dishes and place them in the plastic bags.

5. As soon as growth is detected on the petri dishes, add some soil to the dishes to help the growth along. After these plants have grown a few inches, plant each of them into pots. Continue to care for the plants and observe their overall health and growth and the quality of their produce.

Results

1. Compare the growth of the seeds that were cultivated in the vermiculite and greenhouse incubator with those cultivated on the seed germination medium. Which plants grew faster? Which seeds look healthier?

2. Did the carrot plant or the green bean plant grow faster when it was cut and placed on the callus initiation medium?

3. Did the final plant clones look healthy? Did the difference in their original growth area affect their outcome?

4. Were the vegetables that were produced from the cloned plants as unblemished as their ancestors? Were they of higher quality than those produced from the control (vermiculite) plants?

5

How Effective Is Beta Carotene in Fighting Cancer in Plants?

Purpose

To determine whether beta carotene has any substantial effect in reducing or eliminating the presence of *Agrobacterium tumefaciens* in plants.

Materials Needed

- sunflower seeds
- beta carotene (vitamin A) solution (5 caplets to 1 pint (0.5 liter) water)
- tap water
- flower pots
- potting soil
- disinfectant
- inoculating needle
- candle or match
- *Agrobacterium tumefaciens* (a plant carcinogen)

Experiment

The sunflower seeds will be divided into three equal groups. Group A will be germinated in the beta carotene solution, while Groups B and C will be germinated in tap water only. After the seeds have germinated, they will be planted in potting soil. Groups A and B will be given the carcinogen and will serve as the experimental groups, while Group C will be carcinogen-free and serve as the control. Group A will then be watered twice a week with the beta carotene solution. Groups B and C will be watered twice a week with tap water. The growth of the plants will be monitored over a two-month period.

Procedure

Divide the sunflower seeds into three groups. Germinate the seeds in Group A in the beta carotene solution and the seeds in Groups B and C in tap water. After the

Draw some *Agrobacterium tumefaciens* onto the inoculating needle.

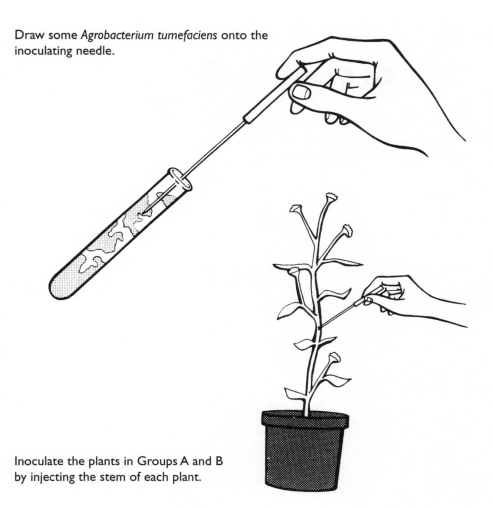

Inoculate the plants in Groups A and B by injecting the stem of each plant.

seeds have germinated, plant them in the flower pots in potting soil. Allow the plants to grow to approximately 7 to 10 inches (18 to 25 cm), after which the plants in Groups A and B will be ready for inoculation.

1. Thoroughly clean the working area with disinfectant.
2. Sterilize the inoculating needle by holding it for 3 seconds in the flame of the candle. Draw some of the *Agrobacterium tumefaciens* culture onto the needle tip and inject the plants from Group A. Then, sterilize the needle once again and inoculate the plants from Group B. Do not inoculate the plants from Group C, because it is the control group.
3. Continue to water the plants in Group A twice each week with the beta carotene solution and the plants in Groups B and C with tap water.
4. Record growth rates of the plants each week and note their appearance and rate of deterioration.

Results

1. Compare the growth of the plants before the inoculation process. Rate the plants according to their amount of growth and general condition.
2. Compare the growth of the plants after the inoculation process. Rate the plants according to their amount of growth and general condition.
3. Do you believe that the beta carotene solution had any effect in reducing or eliminating the disease in Group A?

6

The Effect of Electromagnetic Fields on *Eremosphaera* Algae Cells

Purpose

To determine if and how electromagnetic fields affect the number and appearance of algae cells at increasingly higher levels.

Materials Needed

- *Eremosphaera* algae colony
- 7 test tubes
- dropper
- slides
- microscope
- graduated measuring cup
- spring water
- masking tape
- marking pen

- electrical wire
- 2-light bathroom bar light fixture
- 2 Gro-Light brand fluorescent bulbs
- wood panel (upright and self-supporting)
- hammer and nails
- wall outlet
- thermometer

Experiment

The algae colony will be divided into seven equal groups and placed into seven test tubes filled with water. Groups 1 through 6 will be placed in an electromagnetic field by being encircled by increasing levels of spiraled electrical wire. Group 7 will serve as the control and will not be exposed to the electromagnetic field of the apparatus, by being placed in another room. The algae will be left within their electromagnetic fields for a period of time and will then be analyzed.

Procedure

1. Divide the *Eremosphaera* algae colony into seven equal groups in test tubes. Observe a droplet specimen from each group on a slide under a microscope. Record the appearance of the cell structures and the amount of cells present in each droplet. Fill each tube with ⅛ cup (30 ml) of spring water. Label the test tubes 1 through 7.

2. Wrap one layer of five coils of electrical wire (connected to a live circuit) around test tube 1, three layers of five coils around test tube 2 (= 15 spirals), six layers of five coils around test tube 3 (= 30 spirals), nine layers of five coils around test tube 4 (= 45 spirals), twelve layers of five coils around test tube 5 (= 60 spirals), and fifteen layers of five coils around test tube 6 (= 75 spirals) (see diagram). Test tube 7 will not be wrapped with electrical wiring.

3. Affix the test tubes below the light fixture equipped with the Gro-Light bulbs, allowing for a 6-inch (15-cm) space between each test tube (with the exception of tube 7 which will be exposed to the normal electromagnetic fields found in another room of your house).

4. Carefully nail the back of the light fixture to the wood panel. Then plug the apparatus into a nearby wall outlet.

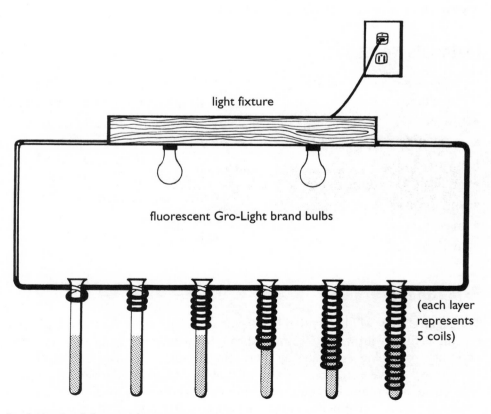

A schematic of the testing apparatus set-up.

5. Leave the tubes exposed for about an hour, then turn off the power and measure the temperature within each vial. Then, take a droplet specimen from each tube again to record your observations of the cell structures and the number of cells within each droplet. Repeat the experiment by exposing the test tubes to the electromagnetic fields for two additional hours and record your observations.

Results

1. Compare the appearance and number of cells found initially in each test tube to those found at the end of the experiment. Did they vary within the same tube?

2. Did cell appearance and quantity change from tube to tube? Were these changes more apparent as higher electromagnetic fields were introduced?

3. Compare the temperatures of all the tubes. At higher temperatures what changes occurred?

7

What Is the Most Efficient Substance for Melting Ice?

Purpose

To determine the most effective of seven substances traditionally used for melting ice.

Materials Needed

- 14 aluminum foil baking pans (8 × 8 × 2 inches) (20 × 20 × 5 cm)
- tap water to fill each pan
- masking tape
- marking pen
- 1 cup (0.24 liter) calcium chloride
- 1 cup (0.24 liter) of a commercial brand of melting crystals
- 1 cup (0.24 liter) sodium chloride
- 1 cup (0.24 liter) cat box litter
- 1 cup (0.24 liter) sand
- 1 cup (0.24 liter) rubbing alcohol
- 1 cup (0.24 liter) mineral rock salt
- large freezer (experiment can be done outside if temperature is below 32° F or 0° C)

Experiment

Fourteen aluminum foil baking pans containing ice will be subjected to equivalent amounts of different substances commonly used to melt ice. Each pan will be timed individually so as to determine which substance, and the way it is applied, is the most effective in melting the ice. Comparisons will then be made between each substance to see the amount of residue each has left and whether that residue could have damaging effects on paved driveways and sidewalks.

Procedure

1. Fill seven of the baking pans with water and freeze them either in a large freezer or outdoors. Label this lot Group A.

76

2. Pour one-half of each of the seven substances separately into the remaining seven baking pans. Label each pan with the name of its substance. Carefully fill the pans with water and place them in the freezer or outdoors to freeze. Label this lot Group B.

3. When the water in Group A has completely solidified, pour the remaining half of each substance into the separate pans. Label each pan with the name of its substance and return them to the freezer.

4. At this point, all 14 pans of water/ice will be in contact with one of the substances. Measure the amount of melting of each pan in Group A in half-hour intervals over a 3-hour period and record your results. Check on Group B in half-hour intervals also, noting the rate of ice formation, if any, over a 3-hour period. Record your results.

5. Pour some of the contents of each baking pan in Group A onto separate sections of a uniformly paved driveway and label. Pour some of the contents of the Group B pans into separate sections of a uniform cement sidewalk and label. Allow all of the water to evaporate. Let the different types of residue stay where they are for 4 to 6 weeks. After this time, sweep them away and note any damage that has resulted. Compare the effects of the same substances on both surfaces.

Results

1. Which substance in Group A melted the ice fastest? How well did this substance prevent the formation of ice in Group B?

2. Did the addition of the ice-melting substances prior to the application of water in Group B slow or prevent the formation of ice? Does this mean that such substances should be applied to driveways and sidewalks when precipitation and freezing temperatures are expected?

3. Did any of the substances' residues cause damage to either the paved driveway or the sidewalk? If so, what type of damage did you observe?

4. In terms of speed, efficiency, and cost, which substance was the best?

8

What pH Level Is Most Conducive to Corrosion in Iron and Copper?

Purpose

To determine the pH level that induces the most corrosion in the least amount of time in iron and copper in the presence of oxygen.

Materials Needed

- 14 glass cups
- hydrochloric acid
- sodium hydroxide
- distilled water
- litmus paper
- 28 test tubes
- iron filings to fill 14 test tubes halfway

- copper filings to fill 14 test tubes halfway
- masking tape
- marking pen
- a narrow plastic scooping tool
- paper towels

Experiment

Fourteen test tubes will be half filled with iron filings and another fourteen will be half filled with copper filings. Each tube will then receive a different solution of hydrochloric acid, sodium hydroxide, and distilled water of varying pH levels. The tubes will be exposed to the various solutions for one month, with the exception that they will be exposed to oxygen daily for 30 minutes. Each sample will be analyzed daily and at the end of the experiment to note its rate of corrosion.

Procedure

1. Fill 14 cups with varying proportions of the hydrochloric acid, sodium hydroxide, and distilled water to achieve pH levels from 1 (acidic) to 14 (alkaline). Test with litmus paper to make sure you have 14 different pHs. (In an acid solution, the paper will turn bright red. In an alkaline solution, the paper will turn blue.)

2. Fill 14 test tubes halfway with the iron filings and label the tubes from 1a to 14a. Fill the other 14 test tubes halfway with the copper filings and label them from 1b to 14b.

3. Pour some of each pH solution separately into the iron filing tubes and some separately into the copper filing tubes. Each test tube should be about three-fourths full.

4. Leave the filings inside their respective pH solutions for about 30 days, but allow the filings to air out by scooping them out of their test tubes and laying them on separate paper towels for 30 minutes each day. Observe and record the changes that take place in each test tube daily.

Results

1. Which pH level induced the most corrosion in the iron filings? In the copper filings? Which pH level induced the fastest rate of corrosion on iron? On copper? How soon after the beginning of the experiment did you observe these changes?

2. Did the higher pH levels induce more corrosion than the lower pH levels?

3. Did the iron and the copper corrode in the same way?

4. Did any of the pH levels appear to inhibit corrosion?

9

How Effective Is Lobster Shell Chitin in Filtering Wastewater Metallic Ions?

Purpose

To test the filtration abilities of chitin; to compare it with charcoal, a common water filter; and to determine how chitin absorbs metals.

Materials Needed

- 6 test beakers
- metals (iron, lead, zinc, iridium, tin, and silver) and solvents for preparing 6 different (100 mg/L metal solutions)
- distilled water
- Standard Methods of Atomic Absorption (can be found in a chemistry book)
- 12 5-inch (12-cm) squares of cheesecloth
- glass tube (open at both ends)
- 6 rubber bands
- 12 ounces (300 g) chitin (obtained by cleaning, drying, and chopping lobster shells into ¼-inch (0.5-cm) pieces) per metal solution
- ringstand and clamps
- funnel
- Atomic Absorption Instrument to measure a solution's metallic concentration
- stopwatch
- glass cup
- 12 ounces (300 g) activated carbon (charcoal) per metal solution

Experiment

Several solutions of metals and solvents will be filtered through chitin and charcoal. The filtration effectiveness of each will be compared by measuring the amount of time it takes for each solution to run through both filters and by measuring the concentration of metallic ions present in the solutions' effluent after they have passed through both filters.

Procedure

1. In six separate beakers, prepare a 100 mg/L solution for each of the types of metals, according to the Standard Methods of Atomic Absorption.

2. Fold one square of cheesecloth into four layers and secure it over one end of the glass tube with a rubber band. Place 2 ounces (50 g) of the chitin into the other end of the tube. Then, attach the tube to the ringstand and place the funnel on the glass tube.

3. Remove 2 teaspoons (10 ml) of one solution, measure its metallic concentration with the Atomic Absorption Instrument, and record it. This will be the control. Pour the remaining solution through the apparatus and use the

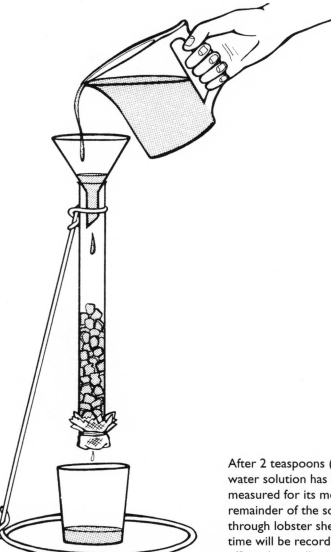

After 2 teaspoons (10 ml) of the metallic/water solution has been removed and measured for its metallic concentration, the remainder of the solution will be poured through lobster shell chitin, and the filtering time will be recorded along with the effluent's metallic concentration.

stopwatch to record the time it takes for the solution to run through the filter and collect as effluent into the cup. Then, test the effluent's metallic concentration with the Atomic Absorption Instrument and record it.

4. Repeat steps 2 and 3 with the other metallic solutions. Whenever a different solution is used, clean the tube and use new chitin, cheesecloth and rubber bands.

5. Then, repeat steps 1 through 4, replacing the chitin with 2 ounces (50 g) of charcoal for each metallic solution.

Results

1. Compare the concentrations of the solutions before and after filtration. What percentage of metal did the chitin remove from each solution? What percentage of metal did the charcoal remove from each solution?

2. Compare the filtration times of the chitin and the charcoal. Does the rate at which a solution passes through either filter affect its metallic concentration?

3. Which metals were absorbed best in the chitin?

10

How Does Saltwater Mix in an Estuary?

Purpose

To determine the average and individual concentrations of salt found in water from various points along an estuary by analyzing the color, density, and residue of the water.

Materials Needed

- 2-quart (-liter) samples of estuary water from seven locations along an estuary
- 250-ml beaker
- 14 test tubes
- 4-quart (-liter) sample of fresh river water (or substitute distilled water)
- 4-quart (-liter) sample of saltwater
- metric graduated cylinder
- 15 plastic cups
- balance scale

Experiment

Three different tests will be used to analyze estuary water. The first test will focus on color variations to distinguish the saltwater from the river water. The second will measure the density of the estuary water to determine the amount of saltwater from the sea that has been mixed in. The third test will measure the residual percentage of salt after the water has evaporated.

Procedure

Test A—To determine visually the average amount of saltwater present within samples from various locations along an estuary.

1. Boil the seven 2-quart (-liter) samples of estuary water separately until each is reduced to 250 ml. Then fill seven test tubes halfway with each of the concentrated samples.

2. Next, make seven saltwater/fresh river water color reference samples in the other seven test tubes with which to compare the concentrated estuary samples. Fill the first test tube halfway with 100% fresh river water, the second with 80% fresh river water and 20% saltwater, the third with 60% fresh river water and 40% saltwater, the fourth with 50% fresh river water and 50% saltwater, the fifth with 40% fresh river water and 60% saltwater, the sixth with 20% fresh river water and 80% saltwater, and the seventh with 100% saltwater (see diagram).

3. Compare the colors of the samples of concentrated estuary water with the colors of the reference samples. For each estuary sample, record the reference sample that most closely resembles it in color.

Test B—To determine the actual amount of saltwater
mixed in by calculating the densities of the seven samples.

1. Using the graduated cylinder, measure 175 cc of each estuary sample into a plastic cup and weigh each cup separately on the balance scale. Then subtract the cup's weight to obtain the mass of each sample.

2. Find the density of each sample by dividing the mass by the volume. Then calculate the average density for all the samples.

3. Next, find the actual percentage of saltwater for each sample. Once you have determined the separate and combined densities of the fresh water and saltwater in your sample and know the sample's total volume, the percentage of fresh river water (x) and saltwater (y) can be calculated as follows:

[(volume of x) (density of x)] + [(volume of y) (density of y)] = total volume × density

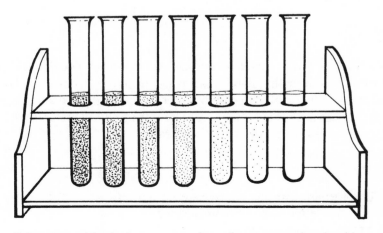

Saltwater and fresh river water color reference samples should be made with which to compare the concentrated estuary samples. Fresh river water is usually several shades browner than mixed river water and saltwater, while saltwater is usually clear.

Test C—To measure the residual percentage of salt in each sample.

1. Pour the remaining estuary samples each into a separate plastic cup. Place another cup alongside and fill it with distilled water until its volume is the same as each of the sample cups.
2. Weigh the cup containing the distilled water on the balance scale and record its mass. Then, weigh both cups on the balance scale and subtract the mass of the distilled water from the mass of the sample water. Repeat for each of the samples and record your results.

Results

1. What were the levels of salt concentration among the samples? Were your color reference samples accurate as to the salt concentrations in each sample?
2. Were the results from each of the three tests consistent for each water sample?
3. Were the salinity levels consistent for all seven locations? If not, which location of the estuary had the highest level of salinity? The least?
4. Experiment with different estuaries. Are the salinity level distributions that you found in the original estuary comparable to those of other estuaries?

11

Can the Life Span of a Soap Bubble Be Extended in Different Temperatures and Atmospheric Conditions?

Purpose

To determine if certain substances can increase the life span of soap bubbles under varying temperatures and atmospheric conditions.

Materials Needed

- 1 cup (240 ml) dishwashing liquid
- tap water
- 3-quart (-liter) glass, metal, or plastic container
- 9 plastic drinking straws
- stopwatch
- 8 clear glass jars with covers
- bubble additives:
  1 teaspoon (5 ml) school glue
  3 drops food coloring

¼ teaspoon (1 ml) vanilla extract
¼ teaspoon (1 ml) witch hazel
¼ teaspoon (1 ml) olive oil
¼ teaspoon (1 ml) aftershave lotion
¼ teaspoon (1 ml) lemon juice

- masking tape
- marking pen
- thermometer

Experiment

Bernoulli's principle of raising and lowering a bubble by changing the air pressure will be tested with bubbles made from liquid soap under two types of atmospheric conditions: a hazy, hot, and humid environment and a clear, cold environment. The same principle will be tested again when the soap bubbles are mixed with bubble additives to see whether the bubbles will be altered in the same two environments. Finally, both types of bubbles will be blown into eight glass jars, covered, and placed in a warm room. The life span of each bubble will be timed until it pops. The same will be done in a cold room. Comparisons will be made between additives under differing temperatures and atmospheric conditions.

Procedure

1. On a hazy, hot, and humid day, mix a solution of ½ cup (120 ml) dishwashing liquid with 2 quarts (liters) water in the container outdoors. Dip one end of a straw into the solution and blow from the other end to create a bubble. Shake the straw lightly to detach the bubble. With a stopwatch, time the life span of the bubble while testing Bernoulli's principle (wave your hand over the

In step 3, after the bubble additives have been mixed into seven of the eight jars, blow a bubble directly inside each jar and time its life span to see which substance holds a bubble the longest in a warm and in a cold environment.

bubble to make it rise, then wave your hand under the bubble to make it sink). Repeat the same procedure on a clear, cold day. Note any changes in the way the bubble forms and the length of time it remains intact.

2. Mix another solution of ½ cup (120 ml) dishwashing liquid and 2 quarts (liters) of water. Pour equal amounts of the solution into the eight jars. Add the specified amount of a different bubble additive to each jar, stir until dissolved, and label each jar. The eighth jar is the control and will contain soap bubbles only. Then, repeat step 1 for the seven jars containing bubble additive and record your results.

3. Bring all eight of the jars indoors. Using a different straw for each mixture, blow a bubble directly into each of the jars. Cover the jars immediately and place them in a warm room heated to 80 degrees Fahrenheit. Observe each bubble and record the time it takes for each to pop. Repeat this step in a room cooled to 45 degrees Fahrenheit. You may also use a refrigerator.

Results

1. Did the air pressure within the plain soap bubbles change under different atmospheric conditions? If so, how did the bubbles react, and how long did they exist under each condition?

2. Did the bubble additives have any effect in changing the way the bubbles reacted to each environment? If so, what were these effects?

3. Did the plain soap bubbles or the bubbles with additives last longer under warmer or colder temperatures?

4. In which bubble additive solution did the bubbles last the longest under all conditions?

5. What practical applications might this experiment have for industry?

12

What Colored Dyes Are Found in Powdered Drink Mix and Colored Marking Pens?

Purpose

To find out which colored dyes are used in powdered drink mix and in colored marking pens.

Materials Needed

- pencil
- ruler
- filter paper cut into twenty 6-by-6-inch (15-by-15-cm) squares
- 10 packages of powdered drink mix, each of a different variety
- tap water
- dropper

- 10 small plates
- stapler
- 20 glass jars with lids (or substitute plastic wrap)
- rubbing alcohol
- 10 differently colored marking pens
- timer

Experiment

Paper chromatography, which separates a mixture into its component pigments, will be used to analyze the various colored dyes present in ten flavors of drink mix and ten differently colored marking pens.

Procedure

1. Make pencil marks ¾ inch (2 cm) up from the bottom on both lower corners of ten of the cut-out squares. Draw a line connecting the marks.

A 6-by-6-inch (15-by-15-cm) square, cut from the filter paper, with the drink mix or marking pen spot.

After the spot has dried, roll the filter paper into a cylinder and staple.

When the cylinder is placed in the center of the jar of rubbing alcohol for 15 to 20 minutes, the spot of drink mix or marking pen will separate into its component color

2. Mix a pinch of each variety of powdered drink mix with a drop of water on each of the ten small plates.

3. With the dropper place a droplet of a different variety beneath the pencil line of each filter and allow them to dry. Label the names of each flavor in pencil.

4. When each paper has dried, staple each into a cylinder shape, with the droplet stain on the outside.

5. Fill ten jars about ½ inch (1 cm) high with rubbing alcohol.

6. Place one paper cylinder into each jar without touching the sides of the jars.

7. Cover the jars with lids or plastic wrap.

8. Leave each paper cylinder in the alcohol for about 15 to 20 minutes or until the alcohol reaches the top of the paper.

9. Remove the paper filters and allow them to dry. You have just made a chromatogram and should be able to see the different colored dyes that make up each of the powdered drink mixes used.

10. To experiment with the colored marking pens, repeat steps 1 through 9, making colored marks on the paper filters instead of using the drink mix.

Results

1. Were there more pigments in the chromatograms of the drink mixes or the colored marking pens? What colors were visible in each chromatogram?

2. What pigments were found most often in the drink mixes? What pigments were found most often in the marking pens?

3. Were the lighter-colored drink mixes and marking pens made up of as many pigments as the darker ones?

4. Which of the component dyes traveled furthest up the filter paper? Why?

5. Were the drink mixes and marking pens of the same color made up of different pigments?

13

Can Mathematical Patterns Be Found in Johann Sebastian Bach's Two-Movement Preludes and Fugues?

Purpose

To determine whether there are any mathematical patterns in the composition of Johann Sebastian Bach's two-movement preludes and fugues.

Materials Needed

- computer with attached printer
- computer spreadsheet software for analyzing data and constructing graphs
- sheet music: *Johann Sebastian Bach, Complete Preludes and Fugues For Organ* by Dover Publications, Inc., 1985

Experiment

For each composition, the total number and frequency of notes, the number and frequency of notes in each line of music, and the number and frequency of notes in each measure will be analyzed, along with the ratios of the number of notes between the various lines of music.

Procedure

1. Count the number of notes in the treble, bass, and pedal lines of each measure in each musical composition. Access the data-analyzing computer software

program and enter this data. Use the software to calculate the total number of notes in each line of music and compose a graphical representation of your data. Print out your graph and visually inspect.

2. Count the number of measures in each musical composition and enter this data into your computer. Again, use the software to compose a graphical representation of your data and print for visual inspection.

3. Use the data entered into the computer to print out individual graphs of the number of notes in each of the treble, bass, and pedal lines of each measure for each work and check for patterns.

4. Use the computer data to calculate the ratio of the number of notes in the treble line of each measure to the number of notes in the bass line of each measure. Produce a graphical representation of these ratios and inspect for any patterns.

5. Use the computer data to calculate the total number of notes in each work and then take the square root of these numbers. Produce a graphical representation of this data and inspect for any patterns.

6. Use the data produced in step 1 and calculate how many times a number appeared as the total number of notes in a measure, for each musical composition. Produce a graphical representation of these results.

7. Compare all graphs for results.

Results

1. Was there a set ratio between the number of notes in any two lines of music? Does Bach use a certain number of notes in some measures more than others?

2. Did the number of measures in the minor key works vary more than the number of measures in the major key works?

3. Were you able to detect any mathematical patterns? Try to expand this experiment to determine if other mathematical patterning possibly exists.

14

Measuring the Brightness of an Incandescent Light Bulb

Note: Conduct this experiment under the supervision of an adult who is experienced in electrical wiring. Exercise caution when testing the light bulbs for prolonged periods of time. The International Science and Engineering Fair has established strict guidelines to which all of its affiliate fairs must adhere. These guidelines involve what is unacceptable for display and operation at an affiliated science fair. It is the responsibility of the student to follow these rules carefully. (See the Foreword and/or contact Science Service, the administrator of the ISEF, for a copy of the applicable rules.)

Purpose

To measure the amount of energy given off by various 60-watt incandescent light bulbs to determine if there are differences between the brightnesses of bulbs from different manufacturers.

Materials Needed

- Solar Project Set by Radio Shack, Part No. 277–1201 (comprised of a solar cell connected with wires to a DC motor)
- 7-inch (18-cm) wooden dowel
- 8-by-8-inch (20-by-20-cm) wooden board
- several 3½-inch nails
- 2 washers
- plastic lid from a coffee can
- mechanical revolution counter
- 9-by-9-inch wooden board
- 6-by-4-inch (15-by-10-cm) wooden board

- 12-by-24-inch (30-by-60-cm) wooden board
- electric wall switch
- electric lamp socket
- 2 electric outlet boxes
- electric cord with plug
- 15 unused incandescent light bulbs including 3 bulbs from 5 different companies (60 watt, 120VAC (standard life)
- stopwatch
- an adult helper

Experiment

A number of 60-watt incandescent light bulbs from different manufacturers will be tested to determine if the brightness of the bulbs can be measured effectively by converting light energy into electrical energy. The energy produced by the bulbs will be converted by a solar cell into electrical energy which will be used to drive a motor that will turn a counter. Readings will be taken from the counter to record the amount of energy generated from each light bulb. The results for each manufacturer's bulb will be compared to determine if all 60-watt bulbs offer the same brightness of light.

Procedure

Construct the light bulb testing mechanism (see diagram)

1. Mount the DC motor from the Solar Project Set onto the end of the wooden dowel.
2. Fasten the dowel to the 8-by-8-inch board with the nail and two washers in a manner that will allow it to pivot. Mount the coffee can lid to the shaft of the mechanical revolution counter in a manner that will allow it to turn the numbers on the counter when moved by the shaft of the motor. Mount the apparatus to the 9-by-9-inch board.
3. On the 6-by-4-inch board, attach the solar panel, which is connected to the DC motor by wires, as shown in the diagram.
4. Assemble the light bulb testing mechanism by mounting both the 6-by-4-inch solar panel unit and the 9-by-9-inch DC motor apparatus to the 12-by-24-inch board, as shown in the diagram.

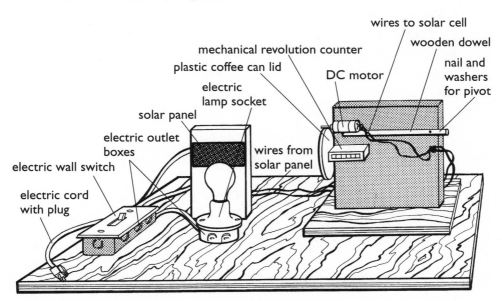

The light bulb testing mechanism ready for experimentation.

5. Complete the unit by mounting the electric wall switch (turns on the light bulb) as well as the electric lamp socket unit to their outlet boxes and onto the 12-by-24-inch wooden board, as shown in the diagram. Attach the electric cord with plug to the electric wall switch outlet box. Since there may not be enough light to drive the motor if the solar cell is too far away from the subject bulb, be sure that the solar cell is placed approximately 1 inch (2.5 cm) away from the bulb.

Test the light bulbs

1. With the light switch in the off position, fasten a light bulb from a particular manufacturer into the light socket.
2. Set the counter to zero and set the stopwatch for 60 seconds.
3. Turn on the light switch at the same time that you start the stopwatch.
4. At 60 seconds, turn off the switch and record the number on the counter.
5. Remove the light bulb from the socket and repeat steps 1 through 4 with the remaining light bulbs from the same manufacturer. Record your data and average your test results for this one manufacturer.
6. Repeat steps 1 through 5 for the bulbs from the other manufacturers. Be sure not to leave any light bulb on for more than three minutes at a time since the sensitive housing of the plastic solar cell could melt.

Results

1. Was there uniformity in counter readings between the sampled bulbs of the same manufacturer? If not, by what margin did the results vary?
2. If there are discrepancies between some of the same company bulb readings, why do you think this is so?
3. Which brand light bulb, if any, offered the greatest amount of brightness as evidenced by your data?
4. Can the brightness of light bulbs be measured effectively by converting light energy into electrical energy?

15

Which Form of Insulation Is Most Effective?

Purpose

To test the effectiveness of various forms of insulation and to determine which would effectively retain the most heat and serve as the best insulator for warming the human body.

Materials Needed

- equal portions of wool, flannel, human hair (can be obtained from a barbershop), thermal insulation, cotton, and chicken feathers (enough to pad both sides of the interior of a plastic bag 1-inch (2.5-cm) thick)
- 7 large plastic resealable bags
- masking tape
- 7 pints (3.5 liters) tap water
- 7 1-pint (0.5-liter) canning jars with lids
- oven thermometer
- 7 total immersion lab thermometers
- refrigerator

Experiment

Seven water-filled jars will serve as models of the human body. The plastic bags filled with insulating materials will represent the insulated clothing being tested.

Procedure

1. Insert one type of insulating material into each plastic bag. Fasten the insulating materials to the insides of the bags with masking tape to equal 1 inch (2.5 cm) thick all around. Leave the seventh bag empty to serve as a control.
2. Boil the water and fill each of the seven jars with equal amounts.
3. Immediately take the temperature of each jar with the oven thermometer and record your data. When the temperature reaches 98.6 degrees Fahrenheit (37

When the temperature reaches 98.6 degrees Fahrenheit (37 degrees Celsius) in each jar, drop a total immersion lab thermometer into each jar and cap it quickly. Then, put each jar into a different insulator pouch.

degrees Celsius) in each jar, drop a total immersion lab thermometer into each jar, and cap it tightly and quickly.

4. Put each jar into a different insulator pouch (including the empty pouch) and place in the refrigerator.

5. Keep the jars in the refrigerator for 2 hours. Take the temperature readings of each jar every 15 minutes and cap quickly after each reading. (Some total immersion lab thermometers have to have their mercury columns shaken down for each new reading.) At the end of the 2 hours, compare readings and note how rapidly they changed over time relative to one another.

Results

1. Was the jar in the control bag colder than the insulated jars?
2. Which insulating material was most effective?
3. Which insulating material was the easiest to work with and would be the most practical in winter clothing? What other insulators could be used in this experiment?

16

Alcohol as a Fuel: Recycling Wastes into Energy

Note: A permit must be obtained from the Bureau of Alcohol, Tobacco, and Firearms before you begin this experiment. It is illegal to make alcohol without a permit.

Purpose

To see if it is possible for a household to construct a simple and inexpensive still capable of recycling its fermented organic garbage into a grade of ethyl alcohol that would meet most of the household's energy needs.

Materials Needed

- 6 feet (1.8 meters) of ⅓-inch (0.85-cm) copper tubing
- coffee can with top and bottom removed
- small bowl
- pressure cooker
- oven thermometer
- 2-gallon (7.6-liter) plastic container
- 1½ gallons (5.7 liters) warm sterile water
- 1 cup (0.24 liter) granulated sugar
- 3 cups (0.72 liter) pureed apple peelings
- sugar hydrometer
- 1 teaspoon (5 ml) active dried yeast
- fermentation lock
- cheesecloth
- proof hydrometer
- ice
- kitchen stove
- 4 fuel-burning lamps
- 16 ounces (0.45 kg) each gasoline, benzene, and kerosene
- adult helper

Experiment

A small portion of sugar and apple peelings will be used to simulate a fraction of a household's weekly organic garbage output. These items will then be combined with water and active dried yeast for distilling in a plastic container. This mixture will be allowed to ferment for approximately 4 to 5 days in a warm, dark environment. The fermented substance will then be placed in a simple pressure cooker still and will be distilled into alcohol. The amount of fuel produced will be measured and multiplied by the weekly output of organic garbage per household to determine the average amount of ethyl alcohol a household could produce. The alcohol will then be tested to compare its burning time and environmental effects with that of more traditional energy fuels.

Procedure

Part I—Build the still.

1. Apply for a permit from the local Bureau of Alcohol, Tobacco, and Firearms to produce a small portion of ethyl alcohol for home fuel experimentation.

2. Begin your experiment by constructing a simple pressure cooker still. With the help of an adult, coil half of the copper tubing five times (leaving the other half extended) and fit the coil within the coffee can so that the end of the coil bends down and out of the bottom of the can into a bowl. Bend the remaining extended copper tubing in an arc over to the pressure cooker. The end of the tubing should hook over the top of the stem on the cooker's lid.

3. Remove the pin from the lid of the pressure cooker and place the oven thermometer in its place. (This will measure the temperature of the alcohol within the pot.) Put the still aside.

Part II—Ferment the organic garbage.

1. Fill the plastic container with the warm sterile water. Add the sugar and the pureed apple peelings. This entire mixture, which is called *mash,* should consist of exactly 20 percent sugar from the table sugar (sucrose) and the sugar found naturally in the apple peelings (fructose). This percentage can be accurately determined by placing the sugar hydrometer into the mash.

2. Mix these items well and add the active dried yeast for distilling to the mash. Cover the container and place the fermentation lock in the lid of the container. The lock will indicate when fermentation has begun and when it has ended. Place the entire unit in a warm, dark environment at around 80 degrees Fahrenheit (27 degrees Celsius) (such as a furnace room) to ferment for about 4 to 5 days. If there are bubbles in the fermentation lock, then fermentation is occurring; if there are no bubbles in the lock, then fermentation has ceased.

Part III—Distill the fermented mash.

1. After fermentation, strain the mash through a cheesecloth, measure the amount of liquid yield, and measure its alcohol proof with the proof hydrometer. Then place the liquid into the pot of the pressure cooker and attach the lid with its copper coil system that you built in Part I. Fill the coffee can unit with ice. Place the still unit onto a stove and heat the contents to about 173 degrees Fahrenheit (78 degrees Celsius) (the temperature at which alcohol boils). Open a window or a vent to provide proper ventilation of the fumes.

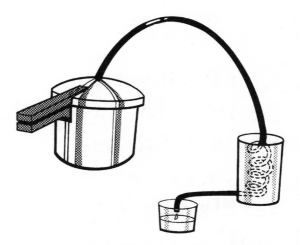

When the contents inside the pressure cooker are heated to about 173 degrees Fahrenheit (78 degrees Celsius), alcohol vapors running through the coils will condense within the coffee can containing ice and come out of the other end of the copper coil into a bowl or cup.

2. During this distillation process, the alcohol vapors running through the coils will condense within the coffee can filled with ice and come out of the other end of the copper coil into the bowl (see illustration). Measure the proof of this alcohol with the proof hydrometer and pour it back into the pot again to be distilled a second time in order to attain an even higher proof. Repeat this process until you have achieved the highest possible proof of alcohol from your still.

3. Measure the amount of alcohol fuel you have produced with the 2 gallons (7.6 liters) of mash. Use this figure to calculate how much alcohol fuel could be produced from what you estimate to be the average weekly household output of organic garbage.

4. Next, prepare four fuel-burning lamps that will each burn the same amount of alcohol, gasoline, benzene, and kerosene individually. Time the longevity of their flames to see which one lasts the longest. Note which one creates the least amount of smoke and odorous fumes.

Results

1. What was the highest proof you were able to obtain in your alcohol?

2. How much alcohol was produced from 2 gallons (7.6 liters) of mash? From your calculations, how much alcohol could be produced weekly from the organic garbage of an average household?

3. Which fuel burned the longest and most efficiently? How long would the average weekly household yield of alcohol last? Would this satisfy most of the household's energy needs? How does alcohol as a fuel source compare to the traditional fuels?

17

Can Earthworms Be Used to Recycle Kitchen Wastes into Fertile Garden Soil?

Purpose

To determine whether it is possible to establish a recycling system for household waste into fertile garden soil by means of earthworms.

Materials Needed

- scale
- 1 colony of red earthworms (approximately 100 worms)
- 3 ounces (84 grams) of cornmeal
- 14 pounds (6.3 kg) of nonfertilized regular lawn soil
- 10-gallon (19-liter) pail
- organic kitchen wastes (e.g., apple peelings, potato peelings, bread crumbs, etc.)
- preweighed container
- latex gloves
- newspaper
- 6 flower pots
- packets of seeds for three types of garden vegetables
- masking tape
- marking pen
- ruler

Experiment

A kitchen compost container will be created to establish and study the feasibility of an organic kitchen waste recycling system that will employ the use of red earthworms. The soil from this system will be compared with that of nonfertilized regular soil for overall quality in growing garden vegetables.

Procedure

1. Weigh the colony of earthworms in the soil that you received them in.

2. Mix the cornmeal into half of the soil in the pail which will serve as the kitchen compost container.

3. Place the worms on the surface of the soil. Once the worms have disappeared into the soil, weigh the unit and place the container in your basement or outside your backdoor.

4. Allow two or three days to pass in which to collect 2 cups (0.5 liter) of organic kitchen wastes. Place the wastes in a preweighed container, weigh the unit as a whole, subtract the weight of the container, and record the weight of the wastes. Add the wastes to the kitchen compost container. Continue to add 2 cups (0.5 liter) of weighed organic kitchen wastes to the compost container every two to three days for a two-month period. In order to determine which types of wastes are more acceptable to the worms, be sure to add a variety of wastes.

5. Weigh the entire compost container at the end of each week and keep a record of its weekly weight. Without disturbing the compost container, check it daily for signs of activity among the worms. Look for young worms and cocoons.

6. At the end of the two-month period, weigh the container and do not add any more kitchen wastes. Put on a pair of latex gloves, take the kitchen compost container into your backyard, and gently empty its contents over newspaper which has been laid over the ground. With your hands, separate most of the

Connecticut Science Fair finalist Frank Waluk and his project.

soil from the worms and divide it evenly between three flower pots. Divide the remaining nonfertilized regular soil between the remaining three flower pots.

7. Germinate the three types of garden vegetable seeds according to the packet instructions and plant some of them separately in the three labeled pots containing the kitchen compost soil. Then, plant some separately in the three labeled pots containing the remaining nonfertilized regular soil.

8. Observe the plants on a daily basis. Once they have sprouted, measure their growth every three days for a period of seven weeks. Note the rate of growth and overall quality of the plants. If time permits, monitor the complete growing cycle of the plants and the quality of the vegetables each one produces.

Results

1. What was the original weight of the kitchen compost container? What was the weight of the container at the end of the two-month period? Subtract the ending weight from the original weight. Does the difference equal the weight of the kitchen wastes that were added over the two-month period, or is it lower?

2. How did the weight of the kitchen compost container vary over the two-month period? Did it increase or remain constant during that time?

3. Was there more activity among the worms during the day or night? Did the worms accept some wastes more than others? What can the activity of the worms tell you about improving upon the kitchen compost container?

4. Which soil produced the best plants? vegetables?

5. Is the kitchen compost container an efficient system for recycling organic kitchen waste? Would the addition of another colony of worms make it more effective?

18

The Great American Lawn and Pristine Water: Can They Coexist?

Note: Safety goggles and gloves should be worn while handling the chemical reagents used in this experiment, which are considered hazardous substances.

Purpose

To determine how the amount of dissolved oxygen in pristine water, which is needed by fish and other water species for survival, is affected by man-made nutrients such as lawn fertilizers.

Materials Needed

- 3 2-ounce (60-ml) water sampling bottles
- distilled water
- 2-ounce (60-ml) water samples from 3 local bodies of water (e.g., lake, pond, and stream)
- 3 gallons (11.5 liters) of water from the same local bodies of water
- latex gloves

- safety goggles
- 6 pipettes
- manganous sulfate solution
- alkaline potassium iodide azide
- sulfamic acid powder
- titration kit
- 3 5-gallon (19-liter) fish tanks, sterilized
- ¼ teaspoon (2 g) each of 3 different lawn fertilizers

Experiment

Water samples from three pristine local bodies of water will be studied in their natural states to determine the amount of dissolved oxygen that they contain. Then, water samples will be drawn from the same bodies of water and transported into fish tanks where various lawn fertilizers will be introduced. These water samples will be studied to determine if the fertilizers have any effect on the amount of dissolved oxygen that was originally found to be present in the samples in their natural states.

Procedure

1. Select three local bodies of water that are situated in rural areas and are secure from possible contamination.
2. Sterilize the water sampling bottles with boiled distilled water before collecting the samples.
3. Fill a bottle with a water sample from each site by submerging it in the water and capping it while still submerged to be sure no air bubbles are trapped inside the bottle. Also collect 3 gallons of water (11.4 liters) from each site.
4. Put on the latex gloves and lab goggles to protect your hands and eyes in this part of the experiment. With a pipette, add eight drops of the manganous sulfate solution to the water sample, being careful not to introduce air into the water sample. With another pipette, add eight drops of alkaline potassium iodide azide to the same water sample, again being sure not to introduce any air into the sample. Cap the bottle and distribute the solution by turning the bottle around several times. After the precipitate forms, let it settle down from the top of the bottle. Add ⅛ teaspoon (1.0 g) of sulfamic acid powder and shake until the precipitate that is formed, as well as the sulfamic acid powder, are dissolved. When the sample becomes yellow- or amber-colored, it is ready for the dissolved oxygen test. Follow the instructions that come with the titration kit that you have obtained, and record the amount of dissolved oxygen for the sample.
5. Repeat steps 3 and 4 for the remaining water samples.
6. Pour one-third of the water that was obtained from the first site into a fish tank. Introduce one-half of one of the lawn fertilizers into the water. Once the fertilizer is dissolved, repeat steps 3 and 4 to determine the amount of dissolved oxygen in the sample and record your results.
7. Repeat step 6 twice, using a clean fish tank each time, to test the two remaining lawn fertilizers with the water remaining from the first site.
8. Empty and wash the fish tanks. Then repeat steps 6 and 7 for the water samples obtained from the second and third sites.

Results

1. Were the amounts of dissolved oxygen found to be the same between the three bodies of water? If not, what factors may have accounted for these differences?
2. Did any of the fertilizers affect the amount of dissolved oxygen originally noted for each sample? If so, would the presence of this fertilizer (in the same proportion as tested in this experiment) have any noticeable effects on the fish and other water species living in any of the tested sites?

19

Do Gas Stations Affect the Soil Around Them?

Purpose

To determine whether gas stations affect the soil around them by comparing the dominant types of soil microbes, as well as the pH level of soil samples, from the land around a typical gas station with those from land away from the gas station.

Materials Needed

- 8-ounce (224-g) soil samples from the land around three gas stations
- 8-ounce (224-g) soil samples from an urban, suburban, and rural area distant from a gas station
- distilled water
- 6 20-ml calibrated tubes with caps
- 6 sterile cotton swabs
- 6 petri dishes: tryptic soy agar with 5% sheep blood

- masking tape
- marking pen
- incubator
- Gram's stain test materials (see Project 37)
- camera
- sterile lab dish with depressions
- pH indicator
- 6 sterile plastic spatulas

Experiment

Soil samples from the land around three different gas station locations will be tested to determine whether bacterial growth from these samples differs from the bacterial growth from soil samples taken from urban, suburban, and rural areas away from the gas stations, which will serve as the controls. Then, the pH levels of the soil samples from the different locations will be determined by performing a pH indicator test.

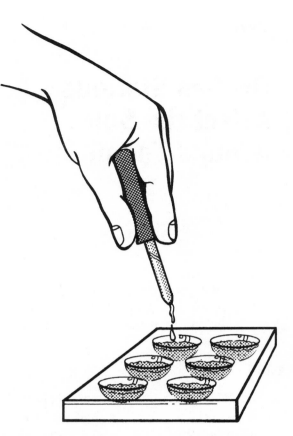

Once each of the soil samples has been placed in the lab dish and labeled, add enough pH indicator to each sample to be able to see the colors that form, and compare them to pH color standards.

Procedure

Part I

1. Place 1 ml of one gas station soil sample in a calibrated tube. Add 2 ml of distilled water and shake for 1 minute.

2. Dip a sterile cotton swab into the tube and streak the swab onto a petri dish. Label the dish and incubate it for 48 hours.

3. Remove the petri dish from the incubator, observe the bacterial growth, and make a Gram's stain (see steps 7 through 10 of Part I in Project 37) from the culture to determine whether the bacteria is gram-positive or gram-negative.

4. Record and photograph your results. Repeat steps 1 through 3 for the remaining gas station soil samples and the control soil samples. Compare your results.

Part II

1. Place a pea-sized portion of each soil sample into a separate depression of the lab dish to cover half the area of each depression, and label all.

2. Add pH indicator drops to each depression so that you can see the color that forms, in order to be able to compare it to the pH color standards (be careful not to flood the depressions). Stir each depression with a sterile spatula.

3. Tilt the lab dish to check the color of all the liquids, and record your pH findings. (The pH indicator will turn red in soil that is highly acidic and will turn blue to violet in soil that is highly alkaline.)

Results

1. Did the bacterial growth in the soil samples from the gas station sites differ from the bacterial growth of the control soil samples? Was the bacteria found to be gram-positive or gram-negative?

2. Which soil samples had the highest and lowest estimated pH levels?

3. What is the overall effect that gas stations appear to have on the soil around them?

20

What Is the Effect of #6 Heating Oil on *Elodea densa* in an Aquatic Environment?

Purpose

To determine the effects of a simulated oil spill on the flora in an aquatic environment.

Materials Needed

- 5 rinsed glass fishbowls
- clean gravel to cover the bottoms of 5 fishbowls
- 10 quarts (10 liters) distilled water
- 40 *Elodea densa* plants
- razor
- ruler
- fluorescent lamp
- microscope
- masking tape
- marking pen
- 500-ml beaker
- 375 ml #6 heating oil

Experiment

The plants will be divided into four experimental groups and one control group. The experimental groups will receive different concentrations of oil, while the control group will receive no oil. The plants will be allowed to adjust to their environments before the oil is administered to them in varying amounts. The reaction and appearance of the plants will be recorded through visual and microscopic observation.

Procedure

1. To each of the fishbowls add gravel to cover the bottom, and 2 quarts (liters) of distilled water.

2. Cut the plants with the razor to 4 inches (10 cm) in length. Separate the plants into five groups, eight plants in each group. Determine the number of stolons (the thread-like growth that branches off the stem) per plant and record the length of each. Record characteristics of color and general health in each plant group. Then, cut each stolon so that any new growth will be detected after experimentation.

3. Place the five plant groups deeply into the gravel of their designated bowls. Make sure that their leaves are not covered.

4. Place the bowls under a fluorescent lamp (each bowl should have the same lighting conditions). Allow the plants to adjust to their environment and root into the gravel for about a week.

5. Once the plants are established in their environment and all of the plants are rooted, begin to cut cross-sections from the plants and observe their inner cell structure under a microscope. Then place one plant from each group on a ruler and measure its average growth in height. Also record any differences in coloration among the plants.

6. Label the fishbowls according to the amount of #6 heating oil they will receive: 200 ml, 100 ml, 50 ml, 25 ml, and 0 ml (the control group). Then, measure the appropriate amounts of #6 heating oil with the beaker and add to each bowl.

7. Expose the plants to the oil for 6 days. Then remove the plants from each bowl and count the number of stolons, if any, and measure the plants to determine the amount of new growth. Cut cross-sections from them to observe their inner cell structure under a microscope. Record the results.

Results

1. At what point in the 6-day period did the plants begin to show any adverse reactions?

2. What changes did you observe, if any, in the cellular structure of the cross-sections before and after the oil was added?

3. Did any stolons reappear in any plant after the experiment?

4. What is the maximum amount of oil per 2 quarts (2 liters) of water that a simulated aquatic flora environment can tolerate and still survive? What does this imply about the fauna that coexist with and depend on such plants?

21

Can Limestone Be Used to Protect Pine Trees from Acid Rain?

Purpose

To determine if limestone, which is used to enrich soil so that grass and shrubbery may grow healthier, could protect pine trees from acid rain.

Materials Needed

- waterproof labels
- marking pen
- 4 potted pine trees [about 2 feet (60 cm) in height and all of the same age]
- 9 ounces (252 g) limestone (can be obtained from a garden supply store)
- tap water
- 3 quarts (2.9 liters) of a simulated acid rain solution (90% water/ 10% sulfuric acid)

Experiment

The soil of two potted pine trees will be fertilized with varying portions of limestone and then sprinkled with the simulated acid rain solution. Two other trees will serve as the controls, with one receiving the acid rain solution only and the other receiving limestone and regular water only. The acid rain solution will be given to the two experimental trees periodically for 4 weeks together with the limestone. The two controls will receive either the acid rain solution or limestone and water only.

Procedure

1. Label the trees as *Experimental 1, Experimental 2, Control 1,* and *Control 2.*
2. Apply ½ ounce (14 g) of limestone to the soil of *Experimental 1,* 1 ounce (28 g) to the soil of *Experimental 2,* and ¾ ounce (21 g) to *Control 1* (no limestone

will be given to *Control 2*). Each tree (with the exception of *Control 1*) will then be sprinkled with 4 ounces (120 ml) of the simulated acid rain solution.

3. One day each week, repeat the same doses of limestone you originally gave to the trees (except *Control 2*). Two days each week, give 4 ounces (120 ml) of the acid rain solution to the trees (except *Control 1*). Give the experimental trees their portion on the same day they will receive the limestone treatments Continue for four weeks.

4. Record the condition of the trees on a daily basis.

Results

1. What were the overall conditions of the plants after experimentation? Were the experimental trees that were treated with limestone in better condition than the control that was not?

2. Did the control that received only limestone and regular water appear healthy or damaged?

3. What combination of limestone (½ ounce or 1 ounce) per 4 ounces acid rain solution yielded the most favorable results?

22

What Section of a Town Has the Most Pollution in the Form of Airborne Particles?

Purpose

To determine which section of any given town contains the most airborne particles as pollution.

Materials Needed

- 30 3-by-5-inch (7.5-by-12.5-cm) index cards
- pencil
- petroleum jelly
- stapler
- 30 sticks of balsa wood or wooden dowels
- magnifying glass
- clear plastic wrap

Experiment

Index cards smeared with petroleum jelly will be used to collect samples of airborne particles from ten designated locations of a town. Three samples will be taken at each location under different types of weather conditions—dry and calm, windy, and hot and humid.

Procedure

1. Select ten test locations in a particular town and write the name of each location on three separate index cards.
2. Draw a circle on the index cards and smear them with petroleum jelly. Next, staple each card to a balsa wood stick and place each stick in the ground at each of the locations for 48 hours under dry and calm weather conditions.

3. After the 48 hours, collect all the sticks and count every particle within the circles using the magnifying glass. Record your results for each location, wrap the cards individually in the plastic wrap and store them carefully.

4. Repeat steps 2 and 3 under windy weather conditions and under hot and humid conditions. (If rainfall should occur, the samples must be retaken.) Record all your results.

5. After all the particle collections are made, average the three results for each location to arrive at a standard number for each particular site.

Results

1. Which site collected the most airborne particles under all three weather conditions?

2. Which type of the three weather conditions seemed to bring about the most airborne particles? The least?

3. Try to identify the airborne particles and their sources.

4. Did the airborne particles that were found in one location appear to be the same as those found in another location? If so, which type of particle seemed to be the most airborne?

5. In general, which section of the town had the most pollution?

23

Environmental Effects on the Biodegradability of Plastic Bags, Paper Bags, and Newspaper

Note: This experiment requires a time period of at least 3 months.

Purpose

To test several types of plastic bags in different environments to determine if and how fast they decompose in comparison to paper bags and newspaper in the same environments.

Materials Needed

- 10 biodegradable plastic bags (use two different brands)
- 10 nonbiodegradable plastic bags (use two different brands)
- 3 nets (plastic or cotton)
- wire or string
- 6 wooden posts
- 5 brown paper bags
- 5 pages of newspaper
- mulch pile—approximately 4 feet (120 cm) high (consisting of grass clippings and leaves with rotting vegetable matter, fertilizer, and compost starter culture) in a 6-foot- (2-m-) diameter ring made of wire fencing material
- tap water
- leaf pile—approximately 3 feet (1 m) high
- 10 plastic containers (approximately ½ gallon (2 liters) each)
- saltwater (15% by volume)

Experiment

The biodegradability of several plastic bags, brown paper bags, and newspaper will be tested in different environmental conditions: in direct sunlight, in a mulch pile (to simulate an active landfill), in a leaf pile (to simulate a dry landfill), in tap water (to simulate a lake), and in saltwater (to simulate an ocean).

Procedure

1. Fold and secure two types of biodegradable plastic bags and two types of non-biodegradable plastic bags on top of a net with wire or string. Tie a wooden post at each end of the net and place each post into the ground, leaving the plastic bags exposed to the sun. Do the same with one paper bag and a page of newspaper.

2. Repeat step 1 by placing the same types of bags in the middle of a mulch pile. Wet the pile thoroughly with water.

3. Repeat step 1 by placing the same types of bags in the middle of the leaf pile.

4. Place two types of biodegradable plastic bags, two types of nonbiodegradable plastic bags, one paper bag, and one page of newspaper into five separate containers of tap water. Then, place the same types of materials into separate containers of 15% (by volume) saltwater.

5. Allow all the materials to stay in their environments for three months or longer. Record the changes that occurred to the plastic bags, paper bags, and newspapers in the different environments upon removal.

Results

1. Did any of the materials decompose? If so, which materials decomposed most thoroughly?

2. Was the rate of degradation greatest in the sunlight, mulch pile, leaf pile, tap water, or saltwater environments?

3. Did the plastic bags that were advertised as biodegradable appear any different from the nonbiodegradable bags?

24

How Does Acid Rain Affect the Cell Structure of *Spirogyra?*

Purpose

To determine whether water that contains a measurable level of acid—with a pH level below 7 (to simulate acid rain)—will affect the cellular structure of *Spirogyra,* a common freshwater algae of the phylum Chlorophyta.

Materials Needed

- 3 *Spirogyra* algae cultures
- 3 1-gallon (3.79-liter) fishbowls
- 6 quarts (liters) distilled water
- 1 quart (liter) soil/water mixture (5 mg soil and 1 quart (liter) tap water)
- 3 lamps, each with 40-watt bulb
- thermometer
- dropper (cc-calibrated)
- concave microscope slides
- 200× microscope
- pH indicator
- 15 cc of 90% water and 10% sulfuric acid

Experiment

Cultures of *Spirogyra* will be grown in three separate fishbowls. One will contain healthy algae cultivated in pollution-free water. Another will contain healthy algae cultivated in a low-acid water solution (water in which a small amount of acid solution is added to bring the pH to a level of 6.0). The third fishbowl will contain healthy algae cultivated in a high-acid water solution (water in which a greater amount of acid solution is added to bring the pH to a level of 3.0). Specimens from each tank will be drawn daily and observed with a 200× microscope. These observations will be recorded and labeled.

Procedure

1. Place equal amounts of *Spirogyra* cultures separately in the three fishbowls which should contain 2 quarts (liters) of distilled water. Then, add an equal amount of the soil/water mixture to each bowl to promote rapid algae growth. Place each bowl under a 40-watt lamp and heat to 68 degrees Fahrenheit (20 degrees Celsius).

2. Observe and record the algae growth daily.

Bowl 1 will be left with the neutral solution of water and healthy algae.

Bowl 2 will contain 3 cc of the water and 10% sulfuric acid solution to yield a low-acid solution with a pH of 6.0.

Bowl 3 will contain 12 cc of the water and 10% sulfuric acid solution to yield a high-acid solution with a pH of 3.0.

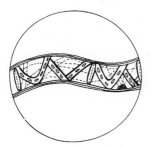 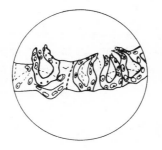 

On day 3, the cell structure of the algae from Bowl 1 should be normal.

On day 3, the cell structure of the algae from Bowl 2 should show some signs of deterioration.

On day 3, the cell structure of the algae from Bowl 3 should be under complete destruction.

3. When the algae appear healthy and abundant, take a sample from each tank and observe it on slides under the microscope. Be sure to label the samples as to the specific bowl from which they were taken.

4. Allow the algae to grow under optimum laboratory conditions for ten days. On the tenth day, take another sample from each of the three bowls and observe them on slides under the microscope. Measure the pH level of the water, using the pH indicator. A neutral solution should be found in each bowl.

5. *Acid Rain Day 1:* The simulated acid rain will now be administered to the bowls. (Bowl 1 will be left with the neutral solution of water and healthy algae to serve as the control.) With the dropper, add 3 cc of the mixture of water and 10% sulfuric acid (to yield a pH of 6.0) into Bowl 2. Into Bowl 3, add 12 cc of the mixture of water and 10% sulfuric acid (to yield a pH of 3.0). Immediately take an algae sample from these two bowls for microscopic viewing, and draw and label the results.

6. *Acid Rain Day 2:* 24 hours after the simulated acid rain has entered the water supply of the *Spirogyra,* take samples of the algae again from each bowl (including the control) and observe them under the microscope. Note any changes in the algae cell structure. Draw and label what you see.

7. *Acid Rain Day 3:* 48 hours after the simulated acid rain has entered the water supply of the *Spirogyra,* take algae samples from each bowl (including the control) and observe them under the microscope. Note any increased cellular changes. Again, draw and label what you see.

8. Compare the differences in the cell structures between the three samples for the 3-day period.

Results

1. Locate a diagram of a typical, healthy *Spirogyra* cell. Is this diagram consistent with your final drawing of algae from Bowl 1? Compare this diagram with your final drawings from Bowls 2 and 3. Were there any changes at all in the structure of the algae? If so, what part of the algae's cellular structure has been altered?

2. What conclusions can be drawn from the effects that the simulated acid rain had on the *Spirogyra?* Was this simulation comparable to actual acid rain? What other acids might be used to simulate the rain?

25

The Presence of Heavy Metals in a Coastal Body of Water and Their Effect on Aquatic Life

An International Science and Engineering Fair Project

Note: This experiment must be conducted under the supervision of a research scientist and x-ray technician. The International Science and Engineering Fair has established strict guidelines to which all of its affiliate fairs must adhere. These guidelines involve experimentation with vertebrate animals and animal tissue. It is the responsibility of the student to follow these rules carefully. (See the Foreword and/or contact Science Service, the administrator of the ISEF, for a copy of the applicable rules.)

Purpose

Since heavy metal pollution in marine environments is a problem in many coastal areas due to the discharge of industrial wastes, the objective of this research project is to determine the type and amount of heavy metal concentrations that exist and how they affect the development and health of fish at different sites along a given coastal body of water.

Materials Needed

- European beam trawl with 60-foot (18-m) line
- various fish species from sites along a coastal body of water
- large plastic freezer bags
- masking tape
- marking pen
- dissection instruments
- large glass lab vials
- 10% buffer solution (formalin phosphate)
- 10% nitric acid

- deionized water
- methylene chloride
- fume hood
- polyethylene scintillation vials with lids
- 120-ml microwave digestion bombs and Teflon liners
- digestive microwave oven

- 50-ml polypropylene centrifuge tubes
- 30% hydrogen peroxide
- flame atomic absorption spectrophotometer (Perkin-Elmer model 2380; AS 50 autosampler)
- X-ray machine
- dissecting microscope

Experiment

Random fish samples will be collected over a period of 12 months from various sites along a coastal body of water. Identification will be made of the species in each of the collection sites; tests for the presence of heavy metals in the fish samples will be conducted through use of an atomic absorption spectrophotometer; and the general health of the sampled fish will be assessed through studying their skeletal structures as well as their stomach and gill contents.

Procedure

Part I—Collect the fish samples.

1. Using the European beam trawl, take tows for five minutes at a time at five miles an hour along designated sites of a coastal body of water you have chosen and collect several samples of fish species (at least three of each species). Repeat procedure at various times during the year to collect a variety of species.

2. Preserve at least two fish from each species collected; place them in separate plastic bags, label the species name, date, and location found, and freeze immediately.

3. Remove the stomach and gills of one fish from each species and place into separately labeled vials containing the 10% buffer solution.

Part II—Dissect the fish and prepare tissue samples; perform atomic absorption spectrophotometry test.

1. Thaw one fish sample from each species.

2. Sterilize instruments before and after dissecting each sample by rinsing them with 10% nitric acid, deionized water, and methylene chloride.

3. With the assistance of a research scientist, perform dissections on each fish sample in a clean fume hood to obtain liver and muscle tissue. Place the tissues into separately labeled polyethylene scintillation vials that have been acid-soaked and rinsed in deionized water. If any fish species are too small for dissection, immerse their entire bodies into the vials.

4. Transfer all the tissue samples (including any whole-bodied samples) from the vials into the Teflon liners and the 120-ml microwave digestion bombs.

Add 1 teaspoon (5 ml) of nitric acid to each sample and allow the samples to de-gas for at least an hour.

5. Seal the bombs and place them in the digestive microwave oven until the samples are digested.

6. Remove the bombs from the oven, cool to room temperature, vent, and transfer the contents of each into separate centrifuge tubes. Then, bring the samples up to the 50-ml mark with ½ teaspoon (2.5 ml) of 30% hydrogen peroxide and deionized water.

7. With the assistance of a research scientist, analyze each prepared sample using the flame atomic absorption spectrophotometer to determine the presence and amount of metals such as copper, cadmium, manganese, zinc, silver, and iron.

Part III—Perform skeletal, gill, and stomach analysis.

1. With the assistance of an X-ray technician, have several radiographs taken of each species group. Analyze and compare the skeletal structures between fish from the same site. Analyze and compare the skeletal structures between fish from different sites. Record your results.

2. Remove the gills from the vials and examine them under the dissecting microscope for abnormalities. Record your results.

3. Remove the stomachs from the vials and check for exterior abnormalities. Then, take tissue cross-sections from the stomach samples and examine them under the dissecting microscope for abnormalities.

International Science and Engineering Fair award winner Nicole D'Amato found that the heavy metal concentrations in her fish samples from Long Island Sound were within the acceptable ranges established by the FDA.

Results

1. What fish species were you able to identify? Were the same species available at the same sites throughout the year?

2. What were the types and amounts of heavy metal concentrations found in the samples? Did they vary in samples taken from the same sites at different times of the year?

3. Did you find any abnormalities in the gills and stomachs of the samples?

26

What Substance Is Most Effective for Cleaning Teeth?

Note: The International Science and Engineering Fair has established strict guidelines to which all of its affiliate fairs must adhere. These guidelines involve experimentation with human and animal tissue. It is the responsibility of the student to follow these rules carefully. (See the Foreword and/or contact Science Service, the administrator of the ISEF, for a copy of the applicable rules.)

Purpose

To determine which tooth cleaner most effectively protects teeth from sugars and acids that dimineralize and decalcify tooth enamel.

Materials Needed

- 12 extracted molars (approximately the same age and in good condition, available from a dentist's office)
- water
- 12 empty petri dishes
- soda pop
- lemon juice
- toothbrush
- baking soda
- mouthwash
- fluoridated toothpaste
- nonfluoridated toothpaste
- tartar-control toothpaste

Experiment

Twelve different molars will be exposed to sugars and acids (soda pop and lemon juice) for a period of three weeks. Each of ten teeth will be cleaned daily with one of the cleaners. The two remaining teeth will serve as the control and will be brushed with water only. At the end of three weeks the condition of the molars will be carefully observed to determine which substance worked the best as a cleaner and provided the greatest protection.

Procedure

1. Rinse the teeth with boiling water and dry them thoroughly.

2. Fill six empty petri dishes three-fourths full with soda pop. Then fill the other six empty petri dishes three-fourths full with lemon juice.

3. Place a molar into each dish, cover it, and label it according to the type of cleaning solution with which it will be brushed. For example, begin by labeling one molar in the soda pop solution *SP—baking soda* and one molar in the lemon juice solution *LJ—baking soda,* and so on.

4. Soak each tooth in its solution for 24 hours. Then remove the teeth individually and brush them with the substance that is labeled on their particular dishes. After cleaning, return the teeth to their petri dishes, cover, and repeat the same procedure daily for three weeks. At the end of the period observe the condition of each tooth. Look for signs of deterioration and discoloring.

Results

1. Did any of the teeth show signs of deterioration and discoloring? If so, what changes did you observe? Were these changes consistent among all the teeth, or did they vary?

2. Which substance, soda pop or lemon juice, had the greatest impact, if any, on the molars?

3. Which substance, if any, kept the teeth clean and protected the longest? Does this result agree or disagree with what your dentist recommends as a tooth cleaner?

27

The Relationship between Alcohol Dosage and Dependency in a Rat

Note: This experiment must be conducted under the supervision of a licensed veterinarian or research scientist. The International Science and Engineering Fair has established strict guidelines to which all of its affiliate fairs must adhere. These guidelines involve experimentation with vertebrate animals. It is the responsibility of the student to follow those rules carefully. (See the Foreword and/or contact Science Service, the administrator of the ISEF, for a copy of the applicable rules.)

Purpose

To determine the effects of various, physically tolerable levels of alcohol exposure in rats by analyzing their behavioral responses and related blood alcohol levels.

Materials Needed

- 4 airtight inhalation chambers
- oxygen and ethanol/oxygen vaporization, metering, and pumping equipment
- food and water for the rats
- 12 laboratory rats
- enzyme assay equipment (for determining the blood-alcohol levels in the rats)
- trichloroacetic acid
- Ependorf tubes
- microcentrifuge
- alcohol dehydrogenase and nicotinamide adenine dinucleotide
- glycine buffer
- timer
- spectrophotometer

Experiment

Twelve rats will be divided into three groups of four and placed individually in air-tight inhalation chambers. Three rats from each group will be exposed to a controlled rate of alcohol vaporization (the experimental group), while the remaining rat will not (the control rat). Over a period of time, blood samples will be obtained from the tail veins of each rat and an enzyme assay test will be conducted to determine the average blood-alcohol level in each rat. After the rats have been exposed for 3 days, they will be removed from their environments. About 6 hours later, the withdrawal symptoms of the rats will be observed for tail tremors, tail stiffening, body tremors, and body rigidity. The experiment will be repeated on Groups 2 and 3 at higher levels of alcohol vaporization.

Procedure

1. Obtain permission to work under the supervision of a research scientist, probably at a local university.
2. Set up the inhalation chambers and connect the ethanol/oxygen vaporization equipment to three chambers, while connecting the fourth chamber to equipment that will vaporize only oxygen. Be sure to supply food and water for each chamber.
3. Place one rat into each of the four chambers and administer the ethanol/oxygen vaporization and the oxygen vaporization.
4. Keep the rats in their chambers with food and water for 3 days. During this period obtain 100 µl of blood from the tail veins of each rat each day with the help of the research scientist and derive the average blood-alcohol level of each rat through the enzyme assay procedure.
5. To complete the enzyme assay procedure, first deproteinize each blood sample by adding 400 µl of trichloroacetic acid to each blood sample in an Ependorf tube. Spin the Ependorf tube for 4 minutes in a microcentrifuge. This will separate the sample into protein and plasma.
6. Place 100 µl of the plasma into a prepared assay vial containing alcohol dehydrogenase and nicotinamide adenine dinucleotide. Add 3 ml of glycine buffer to the vial. Invert the vial and allow it to sit for 30 minutes.
7. Place the vial in a spectrophotometer and set the visible light wavelength to 340 nm. The higher the alcohol content in the vial, the lower the light emission when placed in the spectrophotometer. These measurements will result in a reading that translates to the appropriate percentage of blood-alcohol level.
8. After the third day, remove and separate the first group of experimental rats and the control rat. Compare all symptoms of nervousness and withdrawal immediately and after a 6-hour period.
9. Repeat the same procedures for the second and third groups of rats. However, Group 2 should be exposed to a slightly higher amount of ethanol vapors than Group 1, and Group 3 should be exposed to a slightly higher amount of ethanol vapors than Group 2.

David Karanian found that even low levels of blood-alcohol were sufficient to generate alcohol dependency in the rats as measured by their withdrawal symptoms over a 3-day period.

Results

1. What physical changes were visible in each rat after alcohol exposure? After 6 hours? Were there any noticeable differences between the experimental and the control groups?

2. What was the average blood-alcohol level in each rat? In a particular group? In the entire experimental group?

3. Were there variations among the blood-alcohol levels of the rats?

4. What percentage of blood-alcohol was needed over a 3-day period in order to generate dependency in the rats as measured by withdrawal symptoms?

5. Do you believe from this experiment that it was the amount of ethanol vaporization administered or the continuous exposure to the alcohol over the 3 days that was related to dependency?

6. Can you apply your findings to humans?

28

How Effective Are Various Items in Protecting against Ultraviolet Radiation?

Purpose

To use an organism such as a bacterium to simulate a human body in order to determine the effectiveness of items commonly used to protect against ultraviolet radiation.

Materials Needed

- sterile cotton swabs
- nutrient broth culture of bacteria (*Serratia marcescens*)
- 5 tryptic soy agar plates with 5% sheep blood (more plates will be needed if more than three items will be tested)

- various items used to protect the body against ultraviolet radiation, such as clothing, sunglasses, and sunscreen lotion
- ultraviolet lamp
- timer
- large lid

Experiment

Tryptic soy agar (TSA) plates with 5% sheep blood will be smeared with the bacteria *Serratia marcescens* and allowed to cultivate. Various items to be tested, such as clothing, sunglasses, and sunscreen lotion, will be placed over the bacteria as a protective covering from the ultraviolet radiation that the plates will be exposed to.

After the nutrient agar plates are covered with the bacteria, items normally used in the sun (such as sunglasses) will be placed on each plate to determine if they can actually protect the bacteria from the ultraviolet rays.

Procedure

1. With a sterile cotton swab, place the culture of bacteria on the entire surface of each of the five TSA plates and allow it to cultivate.

2. Cover the entire surface (if possible) of the three experimental plates with the items being tested—for example, clothing, glasses, and sunscreen. To do the sunscreen test, first smear the lotion on clear plastic wrap and then wrap the plastic over the plate. Leave two plates uncovered to serve as the control (one plate will be unexposed to the ultraviolet lamp, while the other will be exposed to the ultraviolet lamp).

3. Place the three experimental plates plus one of the uncovered control plates directly underneath the ultraviolet lamp for 5 minutes of exposure. Then turn off the light and remove the coverings from each dish. Cover these four exposed plates and the unexposed plate with a lid and put the plates away in a dark area at room temperature overnight.

4. Observe the condition of the bacteria after 24 hours and record your observations.

Results

1. Compare the population and color of the bacteria on the experimental plates exposed to ultraviolet light to that of the control plates. Is there any difference between the protected and exposed plates, or between the unprotected/exposed and unprotected/unexposed plates?

2. Which item offered the most protection against ultraviolet radiation? Which offered the least?

3. Compare colored and colorless testing items. Did the colored items have any effect on ultraviolet penetration? Compare the thickness of the materials. Did

thicker testing materials offer better protection against the ultraviolet radiation than thinner materials?

4. Did the sunscreen lotion offer good protection? Based on the data from this experiment, do you think that most people are well protected against ultraviolet radiation?

29

The Wave, the Golden Mean, and $r = \left[\dfrac{2}{\left(-1+\sqrt{5}\right)}\right]^{\wedge}\theta$

An International Science and Engineering Fair Project

Note: Knowledge and experience in analytical geometry, origami, and computer programming are required for this project.

Purpose

To determine if there is any possible relationship between the origami fold known as the "wave" and the Golden Mean or Ratio, the numerical value of which is $\left(\dfrac{1+\sqrt{5}}{2}\right)$. This will be accomplished by determining the equation of the wave's spirals.

Materials Needed

- several sheets of 1-foot- (30-cm-) square origami paper (or more)
- 1 sheet of 20-inch- (50-cm-) square origami paper
- ruler
- 2 sheets of graph paper
- personal computer with 2 megabytes of memory
- software for writing a program that will create and calculate geometric and trigonometric figures and calculations

Experiment

The origami paper will be folded into patterns known as "waves." Each pattern will use a different number of divisions to demonstrate the effects of this on the resulting model. A geometric analysis will be performed to derive equations that describe characteristics of the folded models. Measurements of the models will be taken to be used as data to be related by polar equations. A basic program will be written on a personal computer with the use of software, to draw polar spirals of the logarithmic or equiangular variety, which will be adjusted to match the spirals found in the wave.

Procedure

1. Fold a smaller sheet of paper following the instructions in the diagram, each time using 3, 6, and 12 divisions. Observe the effect this has on the resolution and shape of the model. Try folding another small sheet with an uneven number of divisions (for example, 16ths at the point, moving to 8ths at the outer edges). Record your observations.

2. Carefully examine the structure of the resulting folds. Derive equations for the angles between consecutive secants of each spiral, as a function of the number of the division from the tip of the "wave," taking the tip to be fold #0. Try to use these equations to determine a polar equation describing the spirals.

3. Practice folding the "wave" a few more times. Then, fold a model using 32 divisions with the larger paper. If necessary, use a ruler to make straight creases.

4. Create a polar axis in the center of one of the sheets of graph paper. Draw a radius every .25π radians of rotation. Taking the point of the "wave" as the origin, trace the outline of the outer spiral of the "wave" onto the paper. Measure and record the radius length along each of the radii previously drawn.

5. Graph the measurements, using the angle as the *x* axis and the radius as the *y*

International Science and Engineering Fair finalist Matthew Green and his project.

The Wave

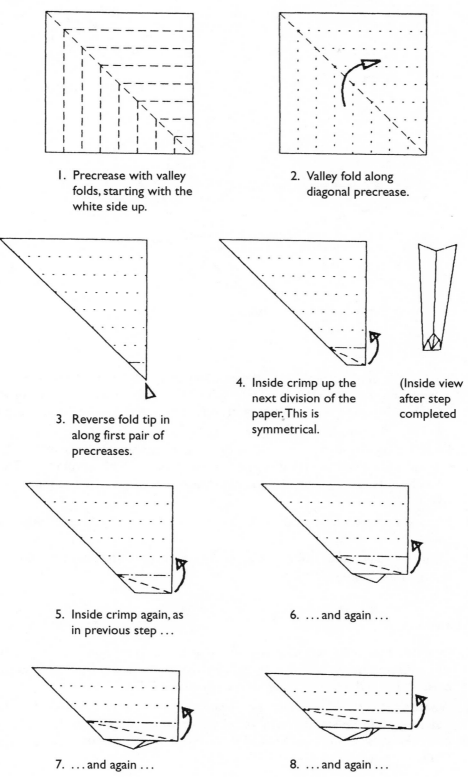

1. Precrease with valley folds, starting with the white side up.

2. Valley fold along diagonal precrease.

3. Reverse fold tip in along first pair of precreases.

4. Inside crimp up the next division of the paper. This is symmetrical.

(Inside view after step completed

5. Inside crimp again, as in previous step ...

6. ... and again ...

7. ... and again ...

8. ... and again ...

9. ...and again ...

10. Valley fold down the flaps.

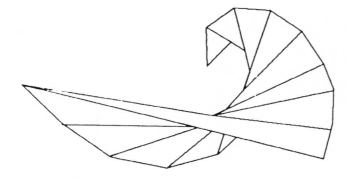

The "wave" model completed

axis, on the graph paper. Using the resulting graph, try to fit the results into an equation. Test the equations by graphing them in the same fashion, or by graphing them as polar equations and comparing the results to the actual spiral of the "wave."

6. Write a program with software that draws polar spirals, with user-definable constants. Include logarithmic spirals as an option. Using this program, adjust the constants to determine the equation that most closely matches that of the spiral of the "wave."

7. Express the best equation in logarithmic form: $ln(r) = k\theta$ and $r = c^{\theta}$, where k and c are constants.

8. Through observation and experimentation, determine the angular rotations between the three spirals.

Results

1. Describe your observations when folding with a different number of divisions and with an uneven number of divisions. What were the results? Was the basic shape of the spiral changed or unchanged? Why?

2. What were the three equations for the angles between secants? Were they the same for all three spirals? Why or why not? Were you able to determine a polar equation from your results? If so, did it show any connection to the Golden Mean?

3. What did the measurements show about the relationship between angle and radius? What type of equation seems to best approximate the measurements? Was there any noticeable relationship to the Golden Mean? What are the disadvantages of using this method?

4. Were you able to find an equation that produced a spiral similar to those in the "wave"? What was the final result? Is there any relationship to the Golden Mean? Can you prove it?

5. What were the rotations between the inner and outer spirals? How could you see this without drawing the graphs? What were the rotations between the outer and middle spirals?

6. What other observations or conclusions can you make? Are there any additional connections to the Golden Mean?

30

Are Dandelions as Effective as Commonly Prescribed Antibiotics against Bacteria?

Purpose

To determine whether dandelion roots, which are used in many parts of the world for therapeutic purposes, can be used as an antibiotic against the bacteria *Serratia marcescens* and *Escherichia coli,* and to determine whether they are as effective as commonly prescribed antibiotics.

Materials Needed

- dandelion roots
- food processor
- cheesecloth
- 5 cups
- sterile distilled water
- dandelion capsules (can be obtained from a health food store)
- sterile pin
- penicillin tablets (250 mg) (can be obtained from a medical doctor)
- Erythromycin tablets (250 mg) (can be obtained from a medical doctor)
- Tetracycline tablets (250 mg) (can be obtained from a medical doctor)
- sterile applicators
- 12 petri dishes: tryptic soy agar with 5% sheep's blood
- *Serratia marcescens* culture
- *Escherichia coli* culture
- masking tape
- marking pen
- incubator
- forceps
- sterile filter paper disks

Experiment

Tests will be carried out to determine whether dandelion roots can be used as effective antibiotics. Dandelion roots taken directly from the ground as well as dandelion root capsules will be tested on selected bacteria to see if they have any effect. Control tests will also be conducted using three common antibiotics as well as distilled water on the same bacteria. The results of both tests will be analyzed and compared.

Procedure

Part I—Prepare the dandelion and the antibiotic tablet solutions.

1. Thoroughly wash several dandelion roots and pulverize them in the food processor until they are liquefied.
2. Filter the liquefied roots through the cheesecloth and into a sterile cup. Add enough distilled water to the liquid to form a one-to-one ratio.
3. Pierce one dandelion capsule with a sterile pin and squeeze the contents into another cup holding ½ cup (0.12 liter) of distilled water.
4. Dissolve one penicillin tablet in ½ cup (0.12 liter) of water. Similarly, dissolve one Erythromycin and one Tetracycline tablet separately into ½ cup (0.12 liter) of water.

Part II—Test the solutions on the bacteria strains.

1. With a sterile applicator, streak six tryptic soy agar (TSA) petri dishes with the *Serratia marcescens*. With another sterile applicator and six TSA petri dishes, repeat this procedure with the *Escherichia coli*. Label the dishes and incubate them for 48 hours at 95 degrees Fahrenheit (35 degrees Celsius). Carefully note the growth of bacteria in each dish.
2. Using the forceps, dip a sterile filter paper disk into the dandelion root solution and place it onto one of the petri dishes containing *S. marcescens*. Dip another sterile filter paper disk into the dandelion capsule solution and place it onto the second petri dish containing *S. marcescens*. Continue this procedure by placing sterile filter paper disks soaked in the three antibiotic solutions onto the next three petri dishes containing *S. marcescens*. Place a sterile filter paper disk soaked only in sterile distilled water onto the remaining dish containing *S. marcescens*. Label all dishes accordingly.
3. Repeat step 2 with those dishes containing *E. coli*.
4. Incubate all the petri dishes for 48 hours at 95 degrees Fahrenheit (35 degrees Celsius). Carefully note the amount of bacteria in each dish and compare those results against the amount of bacteria found in each dish before it was treated. Compare the amount of bacteria between those dishes treated with the dandelion solutions to those treated with the antibiotic solutions and the untreated dishes. Record your observations.

After the dandelion roots are separated from the flowers and stems, wash them thoroughly and pulverize them in the food processor.

Results

1. Were either the dandelion root or capsule solutions effective in inhibiting bacterial growth? If so, did their effectiveness vary with the type of bacteria used? Was one dandelion solution more effective than the other?

2. Were the antibiotic tablets successful in inhibiting the growth of the bacteria used in the experiment?

3. How did the dandelion solutions compare to the antibiotic solutions?

31

Can Food Molds Be Used to Reduce Bacteria Spread by a Pet Rabbit?

Note: This experiment must be conducted under the supervision of a licensed veterinarian or research scientist. The International Science and Engineering Fair has established strict guidelines to which all of its affiliate fairs must adhere. These guidelines involve experimentation with vertebrate animals. It is the responsibility of the student to follow these rules carefully. (See the Foreword and/or contact Science Service, administrator of the ISEF, for a copy of the applicable rules.)

Purpose

To determine if food molds can control the growth of different types of bacteria taken from a pet rabbit.

Materials Needed

- white bread
- plastic bags
- fruit (e.g., cantaloupe)
- Roquefort cheese
- sterile applicators
- bacteria samples taken from a pet rabbit's ears, eyes, and feces
- 15 petri dishes: tryptic soy agar with 5% sheep blood
- masking tape
- marking pen
- 12 sterile spatulas
- antibacterial soap
- incubator

Experiment

Bacteria cultures from the ears, eyes, and feces of a pet rabbit will be analyzed and treated with various food molds to see if the molds can stop the growth of the bacteria. Part of the cultures will also be treated with antibacterial soap only and will be left alone to serve as the controls.

Procedure

1. Take several pieces of white bread, dampen lightly, and put them into a plastic bag. Similarly, cut a piece of fruit (such as a cantaloupe), in half and place one half into a plastic bag. Put the Roquefort cheese aside. Keep all of the food in a warm location and allow it to grow mold.

2. With the help of a licensed veterinarian or research scientist, obtain a bacteria sample with a sterile applicator from around one of the rabbit's ears and streak it onto five of the petri dishes. Repeat the procedure with samples from under the rabbit's eyes and from the rabbit's feces. Label all 15 dishes accordingly.

3. With one of the spatulas, evenly apply a layer of the mold from the white bread to cover the bacteria sample taken from around the rabbit's ear. Repeat the procedure for the samples taken from the rabbit's eyes and feces. Repeat the entire procedure using the molds taken from the fruit and the Roquefort cheese. Three of the six remaining samples will not be treated and will serve as the control set. The last samples will be treated with antibacterial soap.

4. Label and cover all petri dishes and place them in the incubator for 72 hours. Remove the dishes and observe the effects of the food molds and the antibacterial soap, if any, on the treated dishes.

Results

1. Did the food molds have any effect at all in preventing the growth of bacteria? If so, which one was the most effective?

2. If the molds were equally effective, which sample did they have the most antibacterial effect on?

3. How did the food molds compare to the antibacterial soap in inhibiting the growth of bacteria?

32

What Substance Is Most Effective for Preventing the Breeding of Bacteria in Waterbeds?

Purpose

To determine whether bacteria are present inside waterbeds and whether commercial waterbed conditioners or other disinfectants are effective in counteracting any organisms that may live inside.

Materials Needed

- large dropper
- test tubes
- water specimens from new and used waterbeds
- masking tape
- marking pen
- sterile applicators
- petri dishes: tryptic soy agar with 5% sheep blood, and MacConkey

- incubator
- API biochemical test manual
- several brands of waterbed conditioners
- several brands of household disinfectants
- warm tap water
- sterile cups
- sterile filter paper disks

Experiment

Specimens will be taken from both new and used waterbeds. These samples will be streaked individually onto separate tryptic soy agar (TSA) petri dishes, incubated, and observed for bacteria. If present, the bacteria will then be streaked onto MacConkey petri dishes, incubated, and observed for the presence of gram-negative bacteria, which will then be identified through the use of an API biochemical test. Following this step, the waterbed specimens will be streaked again onto another group of TSA petri dishes, and sterile filter paper disks that have each been dipped into a different type of waterbed conditioner and disinfectant will be placed on top of the dishes. The petri dishes will be incubated for 48 hours, and the effectiveness of the conditioners and disinfectants will be assessed.

Procedure

1. Using a large dropper and test tubes, collect water samples from inside several waterbeds and label them to indicate the age and make of each bed they were taken from. Using a sterile applicator, streak a portion of each onto a separate TSA petri dish, cover, label, and incubate them for 48 hours to determine if and how much bacteria are present. Compare and record your observations. If bacteria are present, streak the bacteria from each particular dish onto a corresponding MacConkey dish to determine the presence of gram-negative bacteria, which will be identified by an API biochemical test. API test instructions can be found in an API biochemical test manual.

2. Streak another portion of each specimen onto more TSA petri dishes. Prepare a solution of each brand of waterbed conditioner and disinfectant by diluting each separately in a solution of 1 part chemical to 5 parts water in sterile cups. Next, dip each of several sterile filter paper disks into a separate solution and place them individually on top of separate dishes (leave one dish untreated to serve as the control). Cover each dish and incubate for 48 hours.

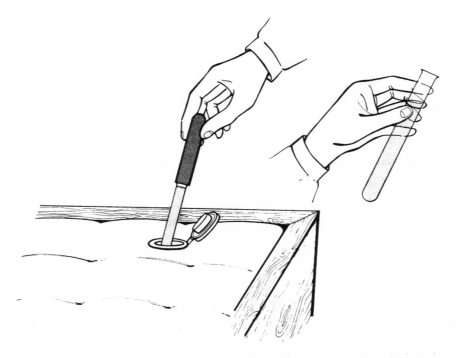

Remove water samples from each waterbed with a large dropper and put them into individual test tubes.

3. Remove the filter paper disks to see if the conditioners and disinfectants had any effect in reducing or eliminating the amount of bacteria that were present. This can be observed by measuring the clear zones found within the area in which the disks were placed on the petri dishes.

Results

1. What types of bacteria were found in the waterbeds? Were any pathogenic?
2. Did the age or make of the waterbeds influence the amount and type of bacteria found in them, or were all the beds consistent?
3. Was the amount of bacteria present in the petri dishes reduced or eliminated as a result of the treated filter paper disks?
4. Of all the chemicals used, which would be the best to keep a waterbed free of organisms?

33

How Can the Amount of Bacteria Found on Kitchen Sponges and Dishcloths Be Reduced?

Purpose

To discover which of several materials used to clean kitchen utensils, and the locations in which this material is kept, will harbor the most bacteria. To determine the measures to be taken in order to reduce most of the bacteria found in the materials after use.

Materials Needed

- masking tape
- marking pen
- 18 petri dishes: tryptic soy agar with 5% sheep blood
- 2 new kitchen sponges
- 2 new dishcloths
- 2 new dish mops
- 18 sterile cotton swabs
- 18 plastic bags
- camera
- 18 soiled eating utensils
- soapy tap water
- boiled water

Experiment

A variety of materials commonly used to wash eating utensils will be tested to see the amounts of bacteria each will contain after use. Several methods of reducing this bacteria before and after use will be tried and compared for effectiveness. The locations in which these materials are kept will also be tested to see which environment is ideal for reducing the amount of bacteria that can be acquired by the materials.

Procedure

1. Label 2 petri dishes for each one of the dishwashing materials. Next, rub a moistened sterile cotton swab across each material and streak it onto its marked petri dish. Cover the petri dishes and put them into plastic bags at room temperature for 24 hours, and then photograph each dish.

2. Divide the soiled utensils into six groups (each group will be washed with a different material). Proceed to wash one group of the utensils with one of the sponges. Then, rinse the sponge with soapy tap water, squeeze it out, and rub another sterile cotton swab across its surface. Streak the cotton swab onto its labeled petri dish, and cover. Then, wash another group of dirty utensils with the other sponge, rinse that sponge with boiled water, and squeeze it out. Rub a cotton swab over its surface, streak it onto another marked petri dish, and cover. Place both dishes into plastic bags at room temperature and photograph each after 24 hours.

3. Repeat step 2 with the remaining groups of utensils and dishwashing materials. Then, analyze each of the petri dishes to determine which material provided the best environment for bacterial growth and which rinsing method eliminated or counteracted the proliferation of bacteria.

4. For the second part of the experiment, place each material in a separate area of your kitchen immediately after being used in the first part of the experiment. (Possible locations include: underneath the sink, on the back of the stove top, on the counter top, and on the back of the sink top.) Allow the materials to stay in their locations for 24 to 48 hours, rub a cotton swab across their surfaces, and then streak each onto a specially marked petri dish. Again, cover the dishes and put them into plastic bags at room temperature. Observe your results.

Results

1. Did any of the dishwashing materials contain any bacterial contamination before they were used?

2. Which material provided the best environment for the bacteria to grow?

3. Which rinsing method appeared to be the most effective in either eliminating or reducing the amount of bacteria present after washing?

4. Did the storage of the sponges, dishcloths, or dish mops have any influence on the amount of bacteria present in the materials 24 to 48 hours after use?

5. What do your results imply about the cleanliness of utensils even after they are washed?

34

An Analysis of the Bacteria and Heavy Metal Content of Sewage before and after Treatment at a Sewage Plant

Purpose

To analyze and compare the bacteria and heavy metal content of sewage from several sewage plants before treatment, and to determine what effects the treatment had on the sewage by analyzing and comparing bacteria and heavy metal content after treatment.

Materials Needed

- sterile wooden applicator sticks
- samples of untreated raw sewage and effluent from several treatment plants
- samples of the same type of sewage and effluent after treatment
- petri dishes: tryptic soy agar (TSA) with 5% sheep blood,

  colistin nalidixic acid (CNA), and MacConkey
- incubator
- API biochemical test manual
- sterile test tubes
- buffer reagent
- dithizone solution reagent

Experiment

Both raw and treated samples of the same type of sewage will be obtained from several sewage treatment plants. TSA petri dishes will first be used to determine the amount of bacteria present in the raw sewage. Then, CNA petri dishes which grow only gram-positive bacteria and MacConkey petri dishes which grow only gram-negative bacteria will be used. API tests will then be administered to identify the types of gram-negative bacteria present. Finally, the presence of heavy metals will be noted with the use of buffer and dithizone solution reagents. The experiment will then be repeated with the sewage samples after treatment.

Procedure

1. Place sterile wooden applicators into each untreated sample, streak them onto individual TSA petri dishes, label, and incubate them for 48 hours. After incubation, analyze the dishes to record the amount of bacteria present.

2. Repeat step 1 using CNA petri dishes, which grow only gram-positive bacteria, and again using MacConkey dishes, which grow only gram-negative bacteria. Incubate the dishes for 48 hours and then record the amount of bacterial growth in all the dishes.

3. Conduct the API tests (you will need to follow the instructions found in an API manual) to identify the types of gram-negative bacteria present in the MacConkey dishes.

4. To determine the amount of heavy metals, if any, present within the untreated sewage samples, put 2 teaspoons (10 ml) of each sample's effluent into individual test tubes. Add 0.1 of the buffer reagent and 1.6 ml of the dithizone reagent to each, and shake vigorously. A noticeable change in the color of the effluents will indicate the presence of heavy metals.

5. Repeat steps 1 through 4 with the treated sewage samples from the same plants. Record, analyze, and compare your results to the untreated samples to see if the bacteria or heavy metal content has decreased.

Results

1. Compare the types of bacteria found at each site. What type of bacteria was the most common among the different plants?

2. Were the bacteria found to be gram-negative or gram-positive? If gram-negative, what types of bacteria were identified?

3. Were heavy metals found in the effluent of any sewage samples? What did this indicate about the types of industries that use the particular sewage plant from which the samples came?

4. Did the treatment of the sewage decrease or alter the state of the bacteria and/or the heavy metals present?

35

Are Your Clams Safe to Eat?

Purpose

To determine if clams purchased fresh from local fish markets—as opposed to those that have gone through a depuration process at a purification plant—are safe to eat.

Materials Needed

- masking tape
- marking pen
- 6 clams each from fish markets in about 10 different regions
- sterile steaming pan
- timer
- sterile knife

- blender (with sterile container)
- sterile applicators
- petri dishes: tryptic soy agar with 5% sheep blood
- incubator
- photographed petri dishes of depured raw and steamed clams (as a control)

Experiment

Clams from different geographical areas that have not been depured will be bacteria-tested in both a raw and a cooked state to observe and compare the fecal bacteria counts to those of photographed petri dishes of depured clams.

Procedure

1. Label the groups of clams as to the areas from which each group came.
2. Take three clams of one group and steam them in the pan for 5 minutes. Then, open them with the knife and put their contents together in the blender; process for 90 seconds.
3. Using a sterile applicator, streak the blend onto a petri dish and incubate for 24 hours.
4. Repeat the blending and streaking procedure using the remaining three clams from the group. Do not steam them.

Brian Curtin bacteria-tested raw and depured clams from different geographical areas to determine if they were safe to eat.

5. Repeat steps 2 through 4 with clams from the other geographical groups.

6. Compare the results from each group to the photographed (control) petri dishes of both raw and steamed clams that have gone through the depuration process at a purification plant.

7. Identify the types and levels of bacteria present, and find out the levels at which they can be safely consumed.

Results

1. How does the bacteria count of the raw clams compare to that of the steamed clams? Did steaming in fact kill the bacteria? Are the raw clams safe to eat?

2. How did the bacteria count of the clams compare from market to market? From market to control (depured)?

3. Were all the bacteria that were found in the clams harmful?

36

Footwear versus Bacteria

Purpose

To determine whether footwear provides an environment for the growth of bacteria, and if so, to discover which type of footwear grows the most bacteria.

Materials Needed

- 10 different types of footwear (one pair from 10 different people)
- sterile applicators
- sterile water
- petri dishes: tryptic soy agar (TSA) with 5% sheep blood, colistin nalidixic acid (CNA), and MacConkey
- incubator
- masking tape
- marking pen
- clock
- camera

Experiment

A variety of footwear worn by ten different people will be used for the first part of the experiment to determine whether significant amounts of bacteria grew during the time they were worn. TSA petri dishes will be used. Then, the type of bacteria that grew most abundantly (gram-positive or gram-negative) will be identified, and the kind of footwear that provided the most ideal conditions for its growth will be determined. This will be done with CNA and MacConkey petri dishes.

Procedure

1. Swab the inside of each shoe or sneaker, before it is worn, with a sterile applicator moistened with sterile water. Streak a separate TSA petri dish with each applicator. Incubate the petri dishes for 48 hours. After incubation, analyze the dishes to determine the amount of bacterial growth. Be sure to label with the names of the individuals who will wear those particular shoes. This procedure will serve as a control for the experiment.

2. After the shoes and sneakers have been worn for 5 hours, swab the inside of each with moist sterile applicators. Then streak each applicator on individual TSA petri dishes. Again, be sure to label the dishes. Incubate the petri dishes for 48 hours and observe them.

3. After incubating the experimental petri dishes, compare them with their corresponding control petri dishes to see whether there were substantial increases in the amount of bacteria present.

4. Swab the inside of the same ten shoes with moist sterile applicators and streak each on CNA petri dishes, which grow only gram-positive bacteria, and on MacConkey petri dishes, which grow only gram-negative bacteria. Again, be sure to label the dishes. Then, incubate the dishes for 48 hours. After incubation, compare the bacterial growth between all the dishes and photograph each dish.

Results

1. Did the use of the footwear for the 5-hour period increase the amount of bacteria present before the experiment?

2. Which type of footwear provided the best environment for the growth of bacteria?

3. Was there any type of footwear that grew little or no bacteria?

4. What type of bacteria grew more abundantly—gram-negative or gram-positive? What does this tell you about the type of bacteria present?

5. What type of footwear seems to be the best to wear? The worst?

Swab the inside of a shoe or sneaker with a moist sterile applicator before it has been worn, and streak the applicator onto TSA petri dishes. Repeat this step after the footwear has been worn for 5 hours, streaking the applicators onto CNA and MacConkey petri dishes as well.

37

The P-Trap:
A Bacteria
Cauldron

An International Science and Engineering Fair Project

Purpose

To investigate the P-trap (the U-shaped pipe located underneath a sink) in various households, to determine:

1. Whether P-traps are vehicles conducive for the growth of bacteria.
2. Whether such bacteria could be harmful to humans.
3. What products could be used to prevent the growth of bacteria at such sites.

Materials Needed

- inoculating loop
- matches
- 20 different household sinks
- petri dishes: tryptic soy agar (TSA) with 5% sheep blood, and MacConkey
- incubator
- clock
- Gram's stain test materials: glass slides, bunsen burner, crystal

violet solution, tap water, iodine solution, 95% ethanol, safranine, microscope with oil-immersion lens
- sterile filter paper disks
- sterile forceps
- a variety of liquid and solid household cleaning products
- API biochemical test manual

Procedure

Part I

1. Sterilize the inoculating loop by passing it through a match flame.
2. Remove the drain plug from one sink.
3. Lower the sterile inoculating loop into the sink drain for 15 seconds.
4. Streak the wet loop onto a TSA petri dish.

Katherine Orzel was a finalist at the International Science and Engineering Fair in Fort Worth, Texas, in 1986 and continued her research on the same topic, receiving finalist honors again at the ISEF in Knoxville, Tennessee, in 1988.

5. Cover, invert, and place the petri dish in an incubator for 48 hours.

6. Wait 48 hours. Remove the petri dish from the incubator, and observe the bacterial growth.

7. Make a Gram's stain from the culture to determine whether the bacteria are gram-positive or gram-negative. This can be done by smearing a colony of bacteria from the petri dish onto a sterile glass slide. Allow the slide to dry, and then warm it by passing it over the flame of a bunsen burner.

8. Then flood the smear with crystal violet solution, and allow it to stand for 1 minute. Next, wash the smear with tap water, flood it with iodine solution, and allow it to stand for 1 minute.

9. Wash the smear again and decolorize it with 95% ethanol until the dye does not run off the smear. Wash the smear again and then counterstain it with safranine for about 30 seconds. Finally, wash it again and allow it to dry.

10. Examine the slide under the oil-immersion lens of a microscope. Gram-positive organisms will be blue, and gram-negative organisms will be red.

11. Repeat steps 1 through 10 with samples from 19 other P-traps.

Part II

1. Streak the TSA petri dishes with water cultures from 20 different P-traps in household sinks.

2. Dip sterile filter paper disks with the forceps into dilutions of the various household cleaning substances and place on the streaked petri dishes.
3. Incubate these petri dishes for 48 hours and observe the results.
4. Repeat the experiment after cleaning the P-traps with the various cleaning substances that appear to be the most effective in counteracting the bacteria.
5. Then, take more cultures from the same P-traps 18 hours later, streak them onto TSA and MacConkey petri dishes, label, and incubate them for 48 hours.
6. Observe the conditions of all the petri dishes, and make a Gram's stain (explained in steps 7 through 10 of Part I).
7. Finally, using an API manual, do an API biochemical test on the MacConkey dishes to identify the type of gram-negative bacteria present in them.

Results

1. Is the P-trap conducive for the growth of bacteria?
2. Does the type of household cleaning substance used affect the growth of the bacteria?
3. Does the length of time that the water stands in the P-trap make any difference in the bacterial growth?
4. What is the best substance to use to clean out the P-trap?
5. Were any of the bacteria found to be pathogenic?

156

38

The P-Trap: A Continuing Dilemma

An International Science and Engineering Fair Project

Note: This project is a continuing study of Project 37: "The P-Trap: A Bacteria Cauldron."

Purpose

The purpose of this second phase of the study is:

1. To compare water from selected P-traps that were investigated previously with samples from the same sites today.
2. To further identify organisms found in the traps.
3. To test for the presence of anaerobic bacteria.
4. To design a mechanism to control the growth of pollutant substances.

Materials Needed

- the same sinks studied in Project 37
- inoculating loop
- matches
- petri dishes: tryptic soy agar (TSA) with 5% sheep blood, and MacConkey

- Gram's stain test materials
- BBL GasPaks
- incubator
- API biochemical test manual
- reverse camp test
- dilution plate test (instructions can be found in a microbiology text)

Procedure

1. Use the sterile inoculating loop to obtain water from one of the P-traps, streak it onto a TSA petri dish, and incubate it for 48 hours. Repeat this procedure using water from the other sites.

2. Make a Gram's stain of all the petri dishes (see steps 7 through 10 in Part I of Project 37). Compare the results with the previous findings.

3. Streak two TSA petri dishes with water from one of the sites. Incubate one in a BBL GasPak and the other in a regular incubator.

4. After 48 hours, take a culture from each dish, subculture them onto separate MacConkey dishes, and incubate for 48 hours.

5. Do Gram's stain and API tests and observe.

6. Repeat Steps 3 through 5 using P-trap water from the other sites.

7. At this point, only facultative anaerobes (organisms that can be grown with or without oxygen) have been isolated from the P-trap (those incubated in the BBL GasPak). Place the TSA petri dishes into GasPaks, seal them, and leave at room temperature for 24 hours to remove the oxygen from the petri dishes.

8. Carry out four additional experiments using the same procedure as in steps 3 and 4, except that oxygen-free petri dishes should be used to isolate the anaerobic bacteria.

9. Use reverse camp tests to identify the anaerobic bacteria from the petri dishes placed in the GasPak.

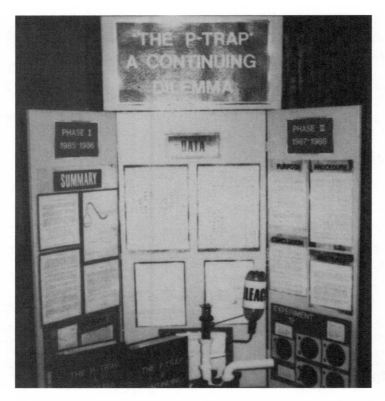

A student can always participate at another science fair with the same topic if he or she has continued research on it or expanded its objective.

10. Use the dilution plate test to determine the number of bacteria colonies, both aerobic and anaerobic, present in the P-traps.

11. Finally, review all of the experiments. Review the piping system and its impact on humans and the environment. Determine what could be done to solve this dilemma, that is, a solution to keep the P-trap bacteria-free (using what you have learned in this experiment).

Results

1. Is there any difference in the amount of bacteria now found in the P-traps with the amounts found previously?

2. How many different types of aerobic bacteria could be isolated from the P-trap?

3. Is there any correlation between the bacteria found in the P-trap and people who use the sink?

4. How long can bacteria remain dormant in the stagnant water of an unused P-trap?

5. How much bacteria, aerobic and anaerobic, was found in any given P-trap?

6. Can some type of mechanism be used in place of the P-trap, or can some device be used to keep the P-trap bacteria-free?

39

Improving the Antibacterial Effects of Garlic

An International Science and Engineering Fair Project

Purpose

To determine whether the antibacterial quality of a garlic plant can be increased by foliar applications of a garlic extract solution.

Materials Needed

- 2 garlic bulbs
- 20 plant containers
- potting soil (enough to fill 20 plant containers)
- sterile distilled water
- masking tape
- marking pen
- knife
- food processor
- cheesecloth
- 3 sterile glass containers
- 2 fine mist atomizers

- *Escherichia coli* bacteria culture
- petri dish: tryptic soy agar (TSA) with 5% sheep blood
- sterile swab
- warm tap water
- isopropyl rubbing alcohol
- dropper
- sterile filter paper disks
- sterilized forceps
- incubator
- thermometer

Experiment

Two groups of garlic plants will be grown: experimental and control. The experimental plants will have garlic extract added to their leaves by a foliar spray, while the control group will be sprayed only with water. The treated leaves will then be pulverized into a solution whose antibacterial effects will be analyzed when applied to a culture of bacteria.

Procedure

Part I

1. From one bulb of garlic obtain 20 cloves (to ensure genetic similarity), and plant one clove into each of 20 plant containers containing potting soil. Add equal amounts of sterile water to each container, watering plants as necessary.
2. Label ten plants "Experimental" and ten "Control."
3. Grow plants until leaves are present and growth is about 6 inches (15 cm) in height.

Part II—Prepare the garlic extract solution.

1. Separate the cloves from the other bulb of garlic and peel them.
2. Pulverize the cloves in the food processor until they are nearly liquefied.
3. Filter the extract by squeezing as much of the liquid portion as possible through cheesecloth into one glass container.
4. Combine one part garlic extract with one part distilled water to make up the garlic spray solution.
5. Fill one fine mist atomizer with the garlic solution. Spray each of the experimental plants with two sprays of the solution, and continue to do so every other day.
6. Fill the other fine mist atomizer with distilled water. Spray each of the control plants with two sprays of the water, and continue to do so every other day.

Part III—Prepare the culture dishes.

1. Transfer the *Escherichia coli* bacteria to the TSA petri dish with a sterile swab.
2. Mark the bottom of the plate into four equal quadrants. Label two sections "Experimental" (A and B) and two "Control" (A and B).

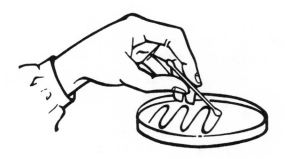

Transfer the *E. coli* bacteria to the TSA dish with a sterile swab.

Part IV—Prepare the test materials from each garlic plant.

1. Cut off the green leaves above the cloves.

2. Thoroughly wash the leaves under warm running water to remove any residue of sprayed materials.

3. Pulverize the leaves of all the experimental plants in an alcohol-sterilized food processor, filter them through cheesecloth into another container, and with the dropper, add three drops of sterile distilled water. Repeat with the control plants. (Keep the mixtures in the sterile containers until they will be used for the zone of inhibition study.)

Filter the pulverized garlic leaves through cheesecloth into the jar, and add three drops of sterile distilled water. This will be done with both the experimental and control leaves.

Part V—Prepare the petri dish for the zone of inhibition study.

1. Soak two sterile filter paper disks in the garlic test solution made from the leaves of each garlic plant (as described in Part IV).

2. With the forceps, place these two filter disks onto the two experimental quadrants of the dish. Place two filter disks soaked in the control plant mixture onto the two control quadrants of the dish.

3. Incubate the dish for 24 hours at 98.6 degrees Fahrenheit (37 degrees Celsius). Measure the diameter of the zones of inhibition in millimeters, and record your data.

Soak the sterile filter paper disks in both the experimental and control filtered leaf extracts.

Experimental A   Experimental B

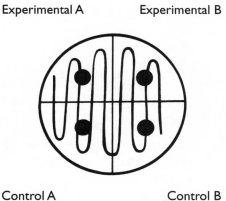

Place the two experimental filter disks onto two sections of the TSA petri dish, and place the control filter disks onto the other two sections for the zone of inhibition study.

Control A   Control B

Results

1. Compare the diameters of the zones of inhibition in the control and experimental groups. Did they differ? How much of a variance existed between the two groups? Which of the two groups had the largest diameters?

2. Which group showed the greatest antibacterial effect? Did the garlic spray affect the antibacterial quality of the garlic plant?

40

Does the Period of Motion of a Pendulum Depend on Its Weight, Amplitude, or Length?

Purpose

To determine if changes in the weight, amplitude, or length affect the period of motion of a pendulum.

Materials Needed

To construct the pendulum frame:

- 2-by-1-inch (5-by-2.5-cm) wood: 5 pieces 2 feet (61 cm) long for the base and top panels and 2 pieces 3 feet (0.9 meter) long for the upright sides of the frame
- 6 small metal angles and screws and/or nails

To construct the pendulum:

- screw hook
- protractor

- balance scale
- fishing weights (minimum 30 units of 1 ounce (0.028 kg) each)
- small plastic bottle with cap
- thin fishing line (minimum 10 feet (3 m))

To measure the variables:

- ruler
- kitchen balance
- stopwatch that can measure to $\frac{1}{100}$ of a second

Experiment

A simple pendulum will be constructed and set into motion several times, with changes made in its variables of weight, length, and angle of release. The average period will be computed, together with its standard deviation, for each experimental run.

Procedure

1. Assemble the pendulum frame using the diagram as a reference. Be sure to attach the screw hook to the center of the upper wood frame. Attach the protractor as shown. Weigh (W) a random number of fishing weights, put them into the small plastic bottle, and attach the cap. Cut a length (L) of the fishing line, and tie one end to the plastic bottle cap and the other to the hook. At this point the pendulum is ready to be set into motion.

2. Bring the bottle to an amplitude of (A) degrees (as indicated by the protractor) from the vertical, and release the pendulum. Time the period of motion (P) with the stopwatch. This is the time between two successive passes of the pendulum through the maximum amplitude. Repeat this procedure (N) times (e.g., ten times) to get consistent results.

3. Compute the average time period (T) and the standard deviation (S):

$$T = \Sigma P \,/\, N$$

$$S = \sqrt{\Sigma(P - T)^2 \,/\, N}$$

where $P(i = 1, 2, \ldots n)$ are the individual measured periods.

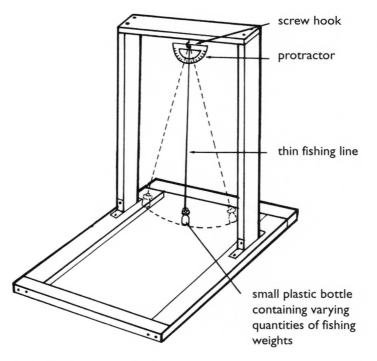

The pendulum set in motion.

4. Repeat steps 2 and 3 with several different values for the three independent variables of length (L), weight (W), and amplitude (A). Select three to five different lengths, from a minimum of about 2 feet (60 cm) to the maximum allowed by the height of your pendulum. Select two or three different weights totaling from about 10 to 30 ounces (0.28 to 0.84 kg). Two or three different amplitudes can also be used in the range of 10 to 39 degrees. (Each run is, of course, characterized by the values of the three independent variables.)

Results

1. Compare the experimental results from all the trial runs with different weights. Did most of the experimental results stay close to the standard deviation (S) of the average period (T)?
2. If not, were the differences significant? Judging from your results, do you believe that the period of motion was dependent upon the weight, amplitude, or length of the pendulum?

41

Are Composites
of Wood Stronger
than Solid Wood?

Purpose

To determine if a wood composite, which is made of a combination of materials that have been saturated with a resin or glue, has greater torsional resistance (twisting) and drop resistance (bending) than a comparable piece of solid wood.

Materials Needed

Testing apparatus:

- 2½-by-2-feet (76-by-61-cm) panel of wood (for test platform)
- metal workshop vise with clamps (to support test bars)
- assorted screws, nuts, and bolts (to fasten the metal workshop horse to the test platform)
- round disk (calibrated in degrees) with attached 4-inch (7.6-cm) arm
- wire fishing line

- spring scale
- several ¼-pound (112-g) lead fishing weights
- ruler

Test bars:

- 10 composite bars (1 foot (30 cm) long by ⅜ inch (1 cm) square)
- 10 solid wood bars (1 foot (30 cm) long by ⅜ inch (1 cm) square)

Experiment 1: Torsional Resistance (Twisting)

Weight will be applied to the wire fishing line from the 4-inch arm at a setting of 4 pounds (1.8 kg) on the attached spring scale. This will move the arrow on the 4-inch arm to measure the degree of twist on the round disk through which the test sample passes (see diagram). This will be done to both the composite and solid test bars.

Procedure 1

1. Set up the test platform as shown in the diagram for the torsional resistance test. In general, this means that a test bar will be held between two clamps

supported by a metal workshop vise. One end of the test bar will pass through a rotating round disk that will measure the arc of twist (in degrees) on the test bar. Attached to the side of the round disk is a 4-inch arm with a hooked wire line that will suspend a spring scale. Various lead fishing weights will be hooked onto the spring scale which will cause the 4-inch arm to move downward while rotating the round disk. This will cause the test bar to twist.

2. Place the composite bar in the holding apparatus.

3. Attach the spring scale to the 4-inch arm. This will automatically place a factor of 4:1 on the scale.

4. Apply force to the wire line by adding weights to the spring scale at a predetermined weight of 4 pounds (1.8 kg). Now, measure the arc of twist on the scaled round disk.

5. Continue to increase the weight at increments of 1 pound (0.45 kg), and measure the arc of twist until the composite wood bar snaps.

6. Remove the composite bar, and repeat steps 2 through 5 with four of the composite bars and five of the solid wood bars.

Experiment 2: Drop Resistance (Bending)

The test bar will be held at one end, and a predetermined amount of weight will be applied at the opposite end, by means of an attached spring scale. The amount of drop resistance will be measured in thousandths of an inch or millimeters.

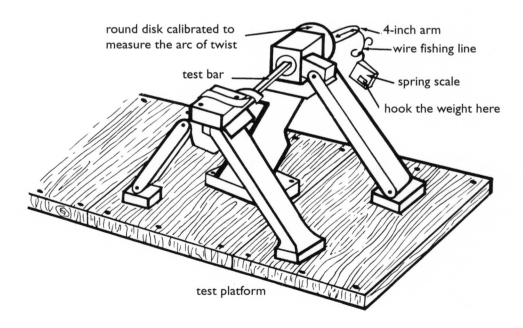

The test platform set up for the torsional resistance test.

Procedure 2

1. Set up the test platform for the drop resistance test. This can be done by removing the side of the vise with the attached round disk and 4-inch arm.

2. Place a composite bar in the remaining holding apparatus and attach the wire line to the opposite end of the bar.

3. Hook the spring scale to the wire line.

4. Apply weight through the spring scale at a predetermined weight setting, and measure the drop of the bar with a ruler.

5. Continue to increase the weight by ¼-pound (112-g) increments, and measure how far the bar drops until it snaps.

6. Remove the composite bar, and repeat steps 2 through 5 with the remaining composite bars and the remaining solid wood bars.

Results

1. Compare the amounts of weight that were needed to move each bar one degree mark when torsional resistance was tested. Which bar proved to be more resistant?

2. Compare the amounts of weight that were needed to snap each bar when drop resistance was tested. Which bar proved to be more resistant?

3. Which type of bar continued to show resistance even after the others had reached their peak resistance?

4. From your experimental results, which bar do you conclude is better at resisting force?

42

Which Angle of Attack Generates the Most Lift?

Purpose

To test four different angles of attack to determine which one generates the most lift of an airfoil.

Materials Needed

- fan
- small wind tunnel [2 feet (61 cm) in length, made of either plywood, balsa, or cardboard] (check with your science teacher for its construction)
- easel clamp
- 4 balsa airfoils of the same dimensions (each glued to the angled face of an airfoil stand)
- 4 balsa airfoil stands with 0-degree, 15-degree, 30-degree, and 50-degree angles cut into one end on each
- balsa wood testing platform
- digital metric scale
- stopwatch

Experiment

Each airfoil will be tested three times, and each test will run for 15 seconds. The 0-degree angle will serve as a control, and the other angles will act as variables. The highest force reading for each airfoil on the digital metric scale is to be recorded at the end of each test. The only variable in the experiment will be the difference in the angle of attack.

Procedure

1. Using the diagram as a general example, set up a wind tunnel testing assembly. Once the unit is set up, do not reposition the wind tunnel or testing platform. If these components are moved, the flow of air around the airfoil will change, and inaccurate results will be obtained.

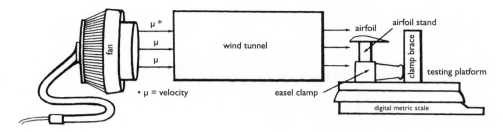

The testing assembly ready for experimentation.

2. Clamp one of the airfoils and its corresponding airfoil stand upright and place it on the balsa wood testing platform (refer to diagram). Then, place the testing assembly on the scale. The leading edge of the airfoil should be parallel to the edge of the wind tunnel's mouth.

3. Calibrate the scale.

4. Immediately after the scale has been calibrated, switch on the fan. Simultaneously, begin timing the first 15-second test with the stopwatch and record the amount of force indicated on the scale. Then repeat this procedure two more times and record the force readings.

5. Repeat steps 2 through 5 three times for each airfoil. Record the highest force reading of the three tests for each separate angle of attack.

6. Graph your results.

Results

1. From the results shown in your graphs, which angle of attack generated the most lift?

2. Why did the angles generate the particular amounts of lift force that they did?

43

Polarization and Stress Analysis of Airplane Windows

Purpose

To discover why airplane windows have an elliptical shape through a process of stress analysis called photoelasticity, and to test other possible window shapes.

Materials Needed

- 2-by-2-by-26-inch (5-by-5-by-66.5-cm) wood frame
- saw
- 6 2-inch (5-cm) squares of felt
- 2 polarizing filters
- 2 ¼-wave plates
- 2 small wooden blocks
- drill
- lamp with 200-watt light bulb (with diffusion coating)
- 35-mm-lens, single-reflex camera
- Lexon plastic (⅛-inch (0.3-cm) thick)
- glass cutter
- 2 metal rods
- 3-kg weight

Experiment

An instrument called a polariscope will be constructed to test the stresses that will occur in differently shaped model airplane windows. The shapes of the windows will be cut out of flat strips of Lexon plastic. These window models will be placed one at a time in the polariscope, while a 200-watt light bulb will shine inside from one end of the polariscope. A 3-kg weight will be loaded onto the model inside the polariscope, and dark, bright bands will appear on the stressed plastic (simulated window). These colored bands, which are called isochromatic fringes, show the stress concentration on the plastic, which represents the stresses that would be around an airplane window. The place at which the fringes are closest together is where the stress concentration is the highest.

Procedure

1. Build a wooden box for the frame of the polariscope (see diagram). The two ends of the box are to be left open. Cut a slot at the top and bottom of the box. Line the slot at the top of the box with felt to prevent light from going around the polarizing filters. Line the inner base of the box with felt, and leave four groove-sized gaps to support the polarizing filters and wave plates. Then, fit the two polarizing filters and wave plates into the slots. Align the two wooden blocks, and drill one hole (for a rod) through both of them. Cover the lined slot at the top of the box with the blocks. Place the lamp and the camera at opposite ends of the polariscope.

2. Cut four pieces of Lexon plastic to 1¾ inches (4.5 cm) in width and 8 inches (20.5 cm) in length. Cut out a shape in each piece with a glass cutter to represent an airplane window. Suggested shapes include: a circle, a rectangle, a diamond, and an elliptical shape (to serve as the control).

3. Drill a hole at the top and the bottom (where the metal rods will be placed) in each strip of plastic. The top rod will hold the model between the two blocks, which will allow the model to be lowered into the polariscope. The bottom rod will load the 3-kg weight onto the bottom of the model.

4. Slide one of the Lexon plastic window shapes through the top slot and insert the metal rods. Then hook on the 3-kg weight.

5. Take pictures of the isochromatic fringes, the color bands that appear near the plastic window opening on the window model inside the polariscope. Different shutter speeds can be used in case the pictures are under- or overexposed. Or you may remove the camera to look through the box end and draw the isochromatic fringes that you see.

6. Repeat steps 4 and 5 with the other window models, and record your results.

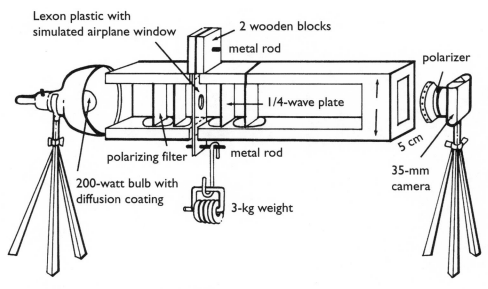

The polariscope set up for experimentation.

Results

1. Analyze the pictures of the models and their isochromatic fringes. Notice where the fringes are closest together. These areas are the points of highest stress concentration. Which areas on each model have high concentrations of stress? Which areas show the least? Why are the fringes arranged in this pattern?

2. Which models overall have less areas of high stress concentration? What explanation can be given for this?

3. Which models are the easiest to produce? Which ones are more practical and easy to use?

4. Based on your results, is the elliptical model the best shape for an airplane window? If not, which model seems to be most effective?

44

Shape and Viscous Effect

Purpose

Spherical objects falling in viscous fluid are known to obey Stokes' Law, in the form of *drag* × *time* = *constant*. The purpose of this experiment is to determine if Stokes' Law would apply to nonspherical objects when dropped in viscous fluids, such as glycerin and corn syrup.

Materials Needed

- plastic cup
- tap water
- metric balance scale (accurate to 0.1 gram)
- 4 ounces (112 g) of glycerin
- 16 ounces (448 g) of corn syrup
- metric ruler
- metal molds (of several shapes)
- modeling clay
- lead fishing weights
- 100-ml graduated cylinder
- stopwatch (accurate to 0.01 seconds)
- 500-ml graduated cylinder

Experiment

Four sets of differently shaped clay objects (suggested are sphere, cube, teardrop, and tetrahedron), all having the same volume but different weights, will be dropped into a 100-ml graduated cylinder filled with glycerin and a 500-ml graduated cylinder filled with corn syrup. These objects will be timed with a stopwatch as each falls from the 100-ml to the 20-ml line in the glycerin and from the 500-ml to the 100-ml line in the corn syrup. Then, the buoyancy, drag, and *drag* × *time* for each object will be calculated. The results will be checked to see if the *drag* × *time* is indeed equal to that of a sphere (constant) which will serve as the control.

Procedure

1. Measure the density of the fluids by filling the plastic cup with water, weighing it on the balance scale, and recording the weight. Do the same with the glycerin and corn syrup. Then, divide the weight of the glycerin into the weight of the

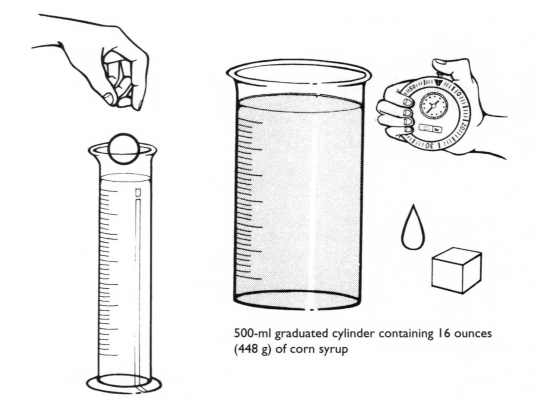

500-ml graduated cylinder containing 16 ounces
(448 g) of corn syrup

100-ml graduated cylinder containing
4 ounces (112 g) of glycerin

Clay objects of various shapes will be timed as they fall through the viscous fluids to see if Stokes' Law applies to them as it does to spheres.

water to obtain the specific gravity of the glycerin. Do the same with the corn syrup.

2. Measure the volume of each metal mold. All clay objects to be made in the same mold will have the same volume.

3. Press clay into the molds. Be sure that the molds are completely filled with the clay.

4. To make clay objects of varying weights, force one or two lead fishing weights in the molds. Scrape off all excess clay (to maintain the same volume). Make an equal number of objects with different weights, but of the same volume, for each shape.

5. Test: Drop one of the spheres into the 100-ml graduated cylinder of glycerin, and start the stopwatch as soon as it hits the 100-ml line. Watch carefully as it glides through the glycerin. The moment it hits the 20-ml line, stop the stopwatch and record the time. Calculate the buoyancy, drag, and *drag* × *time* as the constant. The buoyancy is the object's volume (submerged in the fluid) multiplied by the fluid density. The weight of the object minus the buoyancy is

the drag. Repeat for each object in the glycerin and then in the 500-ml graduated cylinder of corn syrup to compare the times for each, and to see if Stokes' Law applies to the differently shaped objects.

Results

1. What was the time "constant" of the spheres dropped in glycerin?
2. How did the times of the cubes, teardrops, and tetrahedrons compare with those of the spheres?
3. From your observations, would you say that Stokes' Law applied to any of the differently shaped objects?

45

What Would Happen to Climate, Weather Patterns, and Life Forms if the Earth Were Cubical?

Purpose

To theorize what effects a cube-shaped earth would have on climate, weather patterns, and flora/fauna life.

Materials Needed

Experiment I

- 2 empty half-gallon milk cartons
- knife or scissors
- baking soda
- water
- white paper
- tape or glue
- world map
- pencil
- metric ruler
- transparency film marker
- sheet of transparency film
- overhead projector
- globe

Experiment I

- hollow plastic ball [approx. 5-inch (12-cm) diameter]
- sharp knife
- empty half-gallon milk carton
- 2 unsharpened pencils with erasers
- 2 thumb tacks
- modeling clay
- small squeeze bottle
- water
- food coloring
- a helper

Experiment 1

A grid will be drawn on a sheet of transparency film and projected onto an upright parallel globe to simulate the sun and to measure the concentrations of sunlight on various points of a spherical earth. The same will be done with a cubical earth, and the results of each will be compared.

Procedure 1

1. Construct a cubical model of the earth by cutting off the bottoms of two empty half-gallon milk containers and fitting them together. (The milk odor can be removed by soaking the cartons in a solution of baking soda and water for about 15 minutes.) Then, tape or glue the white paper to the cube. Refer to the world map and draw the continents and oceans onto the cube as you think they might appear.

2. Use the metric ruler and the transparency film marker to make a grid on the clear sheet of transparency film, with each square measuring 1 cc. Next, place the grid onto the overhead projector and beam the grid image onto an upright globe that is positioned parallel with the projector.

3. Locate a grid square beaming directly at a place near the 45-degree latitude mark on the globe. Outline the shape directly on the globe. Repeat this procedure, locating a grid shape directly below the first, but at a place near the equator. Measure the length and width of each outlined shape, calculate its area, and note the concentration of light in each. This will simulate the angles at which sunlight strikes the earth's spherical surface and the amount of light concentration at each angle.

4. Repeat step 3 using the cubical earth. For the 45-degree mark, measure one-fourth of the distance into the center of the light-exposed side. For the equator, measure halfway into the center of the light-exposed side.

Results 1

Compare the grid areas of the spherical earth to those of the cubical earth. Were there any differences in the way the simulated sunlight was concentrated on the different outlined points? If so, what do you think the overall climate of the cubical earth would be like?

Experiment 2

Cut a half-sphere out of a hollow plastic ball and a half-cube out of the bottom of a half-gallon milk container. Each will be tacked loosely to the eraser tops of two pencils so that they may spin freely. Then, each pencil unit will stand straight up in a lump of modeling clay. As the half-sphere and half-cube are spun, a steady stream of liquid will be squeezed over their surface. This procedure will theoretically compare and contrast weather systems between a spherical earth and a cubical earth.

Procedure 2

1. Cut the ball in half. Then cut out a cube from the bottom of the empty milk container. Tack the centers of each loosely to the eraser tops of two pencils. Stand each pencil unit straight up in its own lump of clay with the eraser end up. Test the half-sphere and cube to be sure that they spin freely without sliding down.

2. Fill the squeeze bottle half full with the mixture of water and food coloring. Then, spin the half-sphere while your helper squirts a steady stream of the colored dye on the half-sphere. Note the pattern made by the dye as it travels off the half-sphere.

3. Repeat step 2 with the half-cube.

Results 2

1. Compare and contrast the concentration of light between the same continent and ocean locations on the spherical earth and the cubical earth.

2. Was there any difference in the dye patterns between the two models?

3. What kind of effects would the angle at which the sunlight strikes a cubical earth, and the way weather systems move across a cubical earth have on its flora and fauna?

46 The Physics of Cheating in Baseball

Purpose

To determine whether cork, sawdust, or rubber balls, when illegally used as fillers in hollowed-out wooden baseball bats, will cause a baseball to travel farther and give it greater speed upon impact, compared to a heavier, solid wooden bat.

Materials Needed

- 4 solid wooden bats (same length and weight)
- vise
- workbench
- safety goggles
- drill
- rolled cork
- sawdust
- rubber balls (1 inch (2.5 cm) in diameter)
- scale
- wood putty
- sandpaper
- batting device (can be constructed with: screws, eye bolts, nuts, a spring, a hinge, two metal straps, 1 2-by-10-by-40-inch (5-by-25-by-100-cm) board, and 1 2-by-6-by-26-inch (5-by-15-by-65-cm) board)
- baseball
- batting tee
- screwdriver
- tape measure
- radar gun to track speed of baseball (may be obtained by permission of local police department)
- an adult helper
- helpers to bat

Experiment

Three hollow wooden baseball bats, one filled with rolled cork, one with sawdust, and one with rubber balls, and one solid wooden bat will be attached to a batting device in turn. Each bat will spring from the batting device and hit the baseball, which will be set on a tee. The distance at which the ball travels as well as its speed when hit by each bat will be measured and recorded to determine which bat has the greatest effect on the baseball.

Procedure

Part I—Prepare the bats.

1. With adult supervision, safety goggles, and the vise, drill through the tip of one solid wooden bat and hollow out a chamber that is 1 inch (2.5 cm) wide in diameter and 8 inches (20 cm) deep. Repeat this procedure for two additional bats.

2. Fill the chamber of the first bat with rolled cork, the second with sawdust, and the third with rubber balls. Weigh each of the filled bats to ensure that they are lighter than the solid wooden bat. Seal the tips of the bats with wood putty. When dry, smooth the tips with sandpaper and weigh each bat again.

Part II—Build the batting device.

1. Attach the end of the smaller board to the top of the larger board with a hinge so that the boards are perpendicular to each other, as shown in the diagram.

2. Connect the coiled spring between the two boards (as shown in the diagram) and fasten with eye bolts. Be sure that the spring is coiled enough so that when the horizontal board is pulled back and released, it will spring forward.

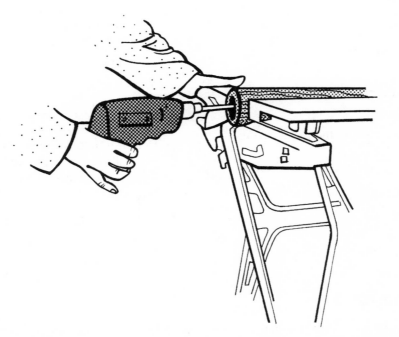

Under the supervision of an adult, drill through the tips of three wooden baseball bats to hollow chambers that are 1 inch (2.5 cm) wide in diameter and 8 inches (20 cm) deep.

Fill the chamber of each hollowed-out bat with cork, sawdust, and rubber balls, respectively.

3. Screw two metal straps to the horizontal board in such a manner that they will support and hold the handle of a baseball bat.

Part III—Test for distance.

1. Transport your batting device, batting tee, bats, and baseball to an open out-door area such as a playing field or park and secure the vertical board into the ground. Unscrew the metal straps on the batting device to attach one of the bats, and reattach the straps to secure the bat in position. Adjust the height and position of the batting device so that the bat will be parallel to the top of the batting tee. Place the baseball on the batting tee, and pull the horizontal board of the batting device back 180 degrees from its resting position and release. Note the exact location where the ball first bounces, and measure the distance from the batting tee to this location. Record your results. Repeat this procedure 25 times for each bat in the batting device at the same angle and tension, to ensure the accuracy of your data.

2. Repeat the test for distance by replacing the batting device with human subjects. Have each batter hit the baseball off the tee a total of ten times with each bat, and measure the distance between the tee and the first bounce. Record your results.

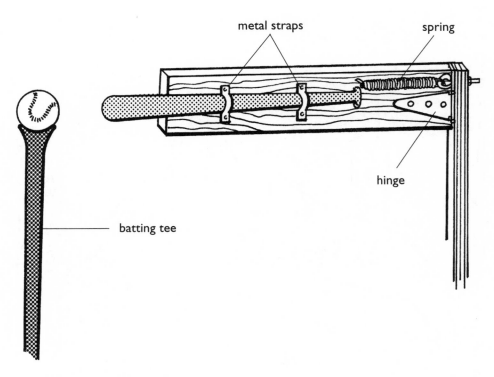

metal straps   spring

hinge

batting tee

The batting device ready for testing.

Part IV—Test for speed.

1. If a radar gun can be obtained, set it up to measure the speed at which the ball travels after being hit by the filled bats and the solid wooden bat. Repeat this procedure 25 times with each bat in the batting device at the same angle and tension, to ensure the accuracy of your data.

2. Repeat the test for speed by replacing the batting device with human subjects. Again, have each batter hit the baseball a total of ten times with each bat, and measure the speed at which the balls travel after being hit from the filled bats and the solid wooden bat.

Results

1. Which baseball bat made the baseball travel the farthest when placed in the batting device? Which baseball bat made the baseball travel the fastest when placed in the batting device? Which variables may have accounted for these results; i.e., was it the weight or the composition of the bat?

2. Did the results of your distance or speed tests vary when human variables were added? If so, in what way?

47

Does a Golf Ball's Bounciness Influence the Distance that It Will Travel?

Purpose

To determine whether the ability of a golf ball to bounce has any relationship to the distance it travels when hit by a golf club.

Materials Needed

- 24 golf balls (3 each of 8 different brands)
- marking pen
- tape measure
- screwdriver
- screws
- 3 2-by-4-inch (5-by-10-cm) wood sections
- saw (use with an adult's help)
- 36-by-36-inch (90-by-90-cm) plywood section that is ¾ inch thick
- 2 eye-lag bolts

- sheet rock screws
- 2 ¾-inch (1.9-cm) plywood sections for corner hinge support and club support
- metal door hinge
- 4-iron gold club head with shortened shaft
- metal door spring ¾ inch (1.9 cm) in diameter and 6 inches (15 cm) in length
- golf tees
- an adult
- a helper

Experiment

A number of golf balls will be tested to determine the height of their bounce when dropped on a hard surface from a set height. Then, the same balls will be hit with the striking mechanism, and the distance to the first bounce of each ball will be measured to determine if the ball that bounces the highest is the one that travels the farthest.

Procedure

Part I—Conduct the bounce test.

1. Group all golf balls by brand name and number each with a marking pen.

2. Select a reference height over a hard surface. A good location would be a brick or cement wall that runs along a cemented or paved surface. Secure the tape measure at the base of the wall and tape it vertically.

3. Have your helper sit on top of the wall, place a golf ball on the edge, and roll it until it drops onto the hard surface. Measure the height of the first bounce against your measuring tape and record your reading. Repeat this step five times with the same ball as well as with different balls of the same brand. Average the bounce heights to obtain a single value for the brand name. Repeat until all of the golf balls have been tested.

Part II—Build the golf ball striking mechanism.

1. Screw one of the 2-by-4-inch wood sections perpendicular to the tops of the other two to form the mechanism's frame. With the adult's help, saw the large plywood section into three parts to form the base and side panels for the mechanism (see diagram).

2. From one of the ¾-inch plywood sections, cut a corner hinge support and attach it to the upper left corner of the mechanism, as shown in the diagram. From the other ¾-inch plywood section, cut a section for mounting the golf club, as shown in the diagram. Attach the door hinge to the club mount section, and secure the 4-iron club head with the shortened shaft. Attach this unit to the corner hinge support, and connect the door spring (see diagram).

3. Position the springed club in its resting position, and align it with a golf tee set on the base.

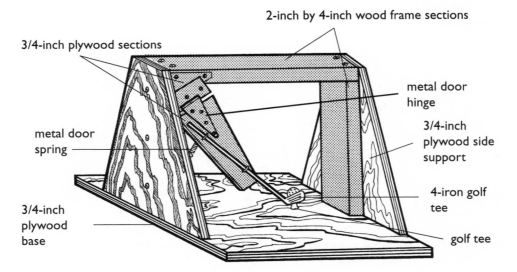

The golf ball striking mechanism ready for testing.

Part III—Conduct the distance test.

1. Transport the golf ball striking mechanism to an open outdoor area such as a playing field or park. Firmly anchor the mechanism to the ground if possible.

2. Place one of the golf balls on the golf tee inside the mechanism, and pull the club unit back to its maximum position and release. Note the exact location where the ball first lands, and measure the distance it traveled. Repeat this step five times with the same ball as well as with different balls of the same brand. Average the distances to obtain a single value for the brand name. Repeat until all of the golf balls have been tested.

Results

1. Did all of the golf balls of the same brand have the same bounce heights? If not, what variables may have accounted for different results?

2. Did all of the golf balls of the same brand travel the same distance? If not, what variables may have accounted for different results?

3. How did all of the brands compare in the bounce test? In the distance test? Does there appear to be a difference in the construction of each golf ball?

4. Which ball bounced the highest? Traveled the farthest? Did the ball that bounced the highest travel the farthest?

48

Relaxing the Breathing Patterns of Newly Purchased Pet Fish so They May Adapt to a New Aquarium

Note: The International Science and Engineering Fair has established strict guidelines to which all of its affiliate fairs must adhere. These guidelines involve experimentation with vertebrate animals. It is the responsibility of the student to follow these rules carefully. (See the Foreword and/or contact Science Service, the administrator of the ISEF, for a copy of the applicable rules.)

Purpose

Because of the drastic environmental changes that occur as a fish moves from a pet shop aquarium, to a plastic bag, to a home aquarium, the immune systems of many pet fish become weakened. Fish tanks are usually filled with tap water that is "bubbly" with oxygen gas. The fish often become sick from the shock and the high amount of undissolved oxygen in their bloodstreams. This experiment will determine if calcium carbonate (a compound that reduces excess gas), when applied to either fish food or fish tank water, has any effect in dissolving the amount of oxygen gas present in the fishes' bodies so that the fish may relax and adapt to their new homes more easily.

Materials Needed

- 3 fish tanks (1 gallon (3.8 liters) each)
- fresh tap water
- 3 fish from a pet shop (of the same breed)
- ½ teaspoon (2.5 ml) of calcium carbonate
- pet fish food (for example, Tetramin brand)
- mortar and pestle

Experiment

One fish will be placed into a tank already containing the calcium carbonate, while another fish will be placed in a different tank and receive the calcium carbonate in its food (experimental groups). A third fish will remain in a tank filled with fresh tap water and plain fish food (control). The fishes will be monitored closely to count their number of gill movements per minute and their level of activity.

Procedure

1. Fill each fish tank with an equal amount of fresh tap water. Then, place all three newly purchased pet shop fish into one of the tanks. For the first minute, record the rate at which their gills move and their levels of activity.

2. Stir ¼ teaspoon (1.25 ml) of calcium carbonate into the second tank. After it has dissolved into the water, place one of the fish into the tank and sprinkle in some plain fish food. Record the fish's gill movements, activity, and appetite.

3. Place a different fish into the third tank. Prepare this fish's food by powdering a serving size of fish food with a mortar and pestle. Then mix ¼ teaspoon (1.25 ml) of calcium carbonate and several drops of water into the powdered food. Mix into the fish tank. Record the gill movements, level of activity, and appetite of this fish.

4. Allow the remaining fish to stay in the original tank. Feed it a meal of plain fish food only. Again, observe its gill movements, activity level, and appetite.

5. Continue to monitor all the fish constantly for the first hour, or until each fish has completely adapted to its environment.

Results

1. How did the fish react when they were originally placed together in the tap water tank? Did they appear different from the way they looked in the pet store? What were the number of gill movements per minute?

2. Did the calcium carbonate appear to have any effect in aiding the fish to adapt to their new environment? If so, which method of administering the compound appeared to be the best?

3. Which fish appeared to have adapted to its environment most quickly? What were its gill movements per minute after it had appeared to relax?

49

Can the Heartbeat of a Chicken Embryo Be Detected without Breaking Its Eggshell?

Note: It is recommended that this experiment be conducted under the supervision of a research scientist. The International Science and Engineering Fair has established strict guidelines to which all of its affiliate fairs must adhere. These guidelines involve experimentation with vertebrate animals. It is the responsibility of the student to follow those rules carefully. (See the Foreword and/or contact Science Service, the administrator of the ISEF, for a copy of the applicable rules.)

Purpose

To see if it is possible to measure the early heartbeat of a chicken embryo without breaking its eggshell or disturbing the chick's development—as other methods have done in the past.

Materials Needed

- Zygo Axiom 200 interferometer
- retroreflector and mount
- VAX computer by Digital Equipment Co.
- 3 3-day-old incubated fertile chicken eggs
- 1 3-day-old dead chicken egg
- incubator

Experiment

The movement within an eggshell will be measured with a Zygo Axiom 200 interferometer (which sends a light from a laser through a beam splitter that splits the light beam in half). One half of that light will travel out to a fixed mirror and bounce back. The other half will travel out to a movable mirror that is touching an egg, so that when its eggshell moves from the embryo's heartbeat, the mirror will also move. Therefore, the beam that will bounce off the movable mirror will have its phase altered in such a way that when it returns to the beam splitter (where it is combined with the other beam), constructive interference will result from the action of the waves joining in phases. Destructive interference will occur if the waves are out of phase. Then, the changes in the distance traveled by the beam going to the egg (in millionths of a millimeter) will be calculated from the patterns of light intensity. The experiment will be repeated on two more fertile embryos (to achieve consistent results) and on a dead embryo (as a control).

Procedure

1. Obtain permission to work under the supervision of a research scientist, probably at a local university.
2. Set up the Zygo Axiom 200 interferometer and the retroreflector and mount with your supervisor's assistance, and connect the apparatus to a VAX computer that will record the data of the changing phases of the beam.

Celeste Peterson found that the interferometer technique was extremely sensitive in picking up the tiny shell vibrations from the 3-day-old chicken embryos without breaking the chicks' eggshells or disturbing their progress.

191

3. Obtain three fertile chicken eggs, together with a dead one (to serve as the control), all of which are about 3 days old. Store them in an incubator. Place one egg at a time gently up against the movable mirror on the retroreflector, and expose it to the light beam for 1½ minutes to collect shell vibrations as data points. Repeat the procedure again when the eggs are 4 and 5 days old.

4. After the data points of the heartbeat frequencies have been sent to the VAX computer, they will be put onto a graph and analyzed as time versus displacement.

5. After experimentation, observe the condition of the eggshells for cracks, and carefully observe the eggs until they hatch, to see if this method has disturbed the chicks' progress in any way.

Results

1. According to your recorded data, what were the average beats per second in each embryo?

2. Were the beats per second less detectable as the embryo matured? Why do you suppose this occurred?

3. Did any of the eggshells crack as a result of experimentation? How long did it take before the eggs hatched? Were the chicks underdeveloped or harmed?

4. What other applications could this method have in studying the development of embryos inside shells?

50

Are Dogs Colorblind?

Note: The International Science and Engineering Fair has established strict guidelines to which all of its affiliate fairs must adhere. These guidelines involve experimentation with vertebrate animals. It is the responsibility of the student to follow those rules carefully. (See the Foreword and/or contact Science Service, the administrator of the ISEF, for a copy of the applicable rules.)

Purpose

To determine if dogs are in fact completely colorblind, as many people believe.

Materials Needed

- assorted colored construction paper
- camera
- black and white film
- 3 glass jars
- 1 dog—any age, breed, or sex, in good health
- dog biscuits or some other treat the dog likes

Experiment

Photographs of colored construction paper will be taken with black and white film to determine how colors appear under varying amounts of light. These pictures will simulate how shades of color would be perceived by a totally colorblind dog. A dog will be trained to consistently choose a jar covered with paper of one shade (as it appears from the photos) from a distinctly differently shaded jar. Once the dog is trained to choose the particular jar, the other jar will be replaced by a jar of a different shade but with similar contrast to the one the dog is trained to choose. The jar positions will be switched frequently to determine whether the dog can still recognize the shaded jar that it was trained to choose.

Procedure

1. Take black and white photographs of an assortment of colored construction paper to determine which colors appear to have similar and dissimilar degrees of brightness and contrast after the film is developed.

After the dog has been trained to choose one jar of a particular degree of brightness and contrast over a distinctly differently shaded jar, color vision will then be necessary when the dog must choose the same jar as opposed to another one with a similar degree of brightness and contrast.

2. Cover two jars with differently colored construction paper that share a similar contrast and brightness when photographed with black and white film. Cover the third jar with another color whose photographed shade is distinctly different from the other two.

3. For the first part of your experiment, the dog will not be tested for colorblindness but will be trained to select one of two similarly shaded jars from the differently shaded one. When the dog can consistently choose the correct jar, reward it with a treat.

4. For the second part of your experiment, replace the jar that the dog was not trained to choose with the second similarly shaded jar. The dog will need color vision to distinguish between the two jars, since with complete colorblindness the two colors would appear to be the same brightness and contrast.

5. Switch the positions of the jars around frequently, and test the dog 100 times. If the dog chooses correctly, continue to reward it to keep it interested. Chart the number of correct and incorrect responses made by the dog in the second part of your experiment.

Results

1. Was the dog able to distinguish between degrees of brightness and contrast in the first part of your experiment?

2. Was the dog consistently correct, incorrect, or did it vary in its responses?

3. Was the dog able to distinguish between the similar shades in the second part of your experiment?

4. Was the dog consistently correct, incorrect, or did it vary in its responses?

5. If the dog was mostly correct, do you think that other variables may have accounted for its accuracy?

APPENDIX A

400+ IDEAS FOR SCIENCE FAIR PROJECT TOPICS

The following list of general science fair project subject areas includes various scientific fields and can be used to find a possible project topic. In addition, the websites of government agencies and scholarly associations may supply you with additional information about these subject areas or explain how to obtain a referral to a local mentor in these subject areas. Many of these agencies and associations have sections on their websites specifically geared toward students and some even sponsor special awards at state and regional science fairs.

A

Acoustics

analysis of sound waves

comparison of acoustic models

comparison of materials used for sound amplification

effects on sound dampening

factors affecting sound pitch

methods of noise control

sound holography

study of anechoic chambers

study of the acoustics of music

For information and contacts on this subject, visit Acoustical Society of America at: www.gbcasa.org

Aerodynamics

analysis of, in vehicles

correlation between wheel diameter and speed

drag study

effect of wind design on velocity and distance

effects of turbulence

wind tunnel design

For information and contacts on this subject, visit NASA at: www.grc.nasa.gov/WWW/K-12/airplane/bga.html

Agriculture

analysis of chemicals used in farming

analysis of pesticides used in farming

analysis of various feeds

comparison of soil types

effect of fertilizers on plant and animal life

genetic engineering in agriculture

soil chemistry and composition

study of irrigation methods

For information and contacts on this subject, visit U.S. Department of Agriculture at: www.usda.gov

Air

effects of aerosols

effects of smog

evaluation of air filters

study of airborne infections

study of air quality in various buildings

For information and contacts on this subject, visit National Oceanic and Atmospheric Administration at: www.arl.noaa.gov

Amino Acids

interaction of, in the body

metabolism of, in the body

method for determining human body absorption rates

Anesthesia

alternative aesthetics

comparison of effects between individuals

side effects of

For information and contacts on this subject, visit American Society of Anesthesiologists at: www.asahq.org

Animals

behavior modification in

communication between

environmental effects on animal behavior

environmental effects on animal migration

genetics and animal breeding

learning in/training of

territoriality in various species

treatment of animal diseases

For information and contacts on this subject, visit American Society for the Prevention of Cruelty to Animals at: www.aspca.org

Antibiotics

analysis of allergic reactions to

comparison of effectiveness between types

sources of

study of bacteria resistance to

For information and contacts on this subject, visit American Medical Association at: www.ama-assn.org

Aquaculture

effects of water temperature and salinity levels on fish hatching

scientific techniques for fisheries

study of algae cultures

study of watershed management standards

use of antimicrobial agents in

For information and contacts on this subject, visit National Aquaculture Association at: www.natlaquaculture.org

Arteries

calcification of

methods for improving arterial circulation

prevention of disease in

study of angiogenesis in

For information and contacts on this subject, visit American Heart Association at: www.americanheart.org

Astronomy

analysis of satellite designs

analysis of telescope designs

effects of cosmic magnetic fields

effects of sunspots on weather systems

predicting the positioning of an object in orbit

study of Doppler imaging of stars

study of the moon's effects on nature

For information and contacts on this subject, visit American Astronomical Society at: www.aas.org

Automobiles

analysis of safety devices for

identification and effects of vehicle emissions

modifications of and improvements in

B

Batteries

comparison of battery types

effects of storage temperatures on

methods for running AC devices on DC power

modifications or improvements in battery chargers

Behavior

behavior modification of children through reinforcement techniques

correlation between handwriting and personality type

correlation between IQ and memory

effects of birth order on social development

effects of classical music on learning

effects of television on social development of children

study of memory retention

For information and contacts on this subject, visit American Psychiatric Association at: www.psych.org

Blood

chemistry and composition of

diseases of

effects on platelet aggregation

effects on the clotting of

regeneration of bone marrow

variations in blood cell counts

For information and contacts on this subject, visit American Association of Blood Banks at: www.aabb.org

Bones

abnormalities in

absorption of calcium supplements by

analysis of fracture types

chemistry and composition of

diseases of

For information and contacts on this subject, visit National Institutes of Health at: www.osteo.org

Botany

biochemical changes in plants in various environments

effects of hormones on plant tissue cultures

effects of soil erosion on plants

external effects on plant growth

medicinal uses of plants

methods for treating crown gall disease

nutrient deficiencies in hydroponically grown plants

plant breeding and crossbreeding analysis

plant cloning techniques

For information and contacts on this subject, visit American Society for Horticulture Science at: www.ashs.org

Brain

abnormalities in

correlation between memory and nucleic acid

diseases of

effects of neurological diagnostic testing

effects of physical injury on

stem cell/spinal cell study

For information and contacts on this subject, visit American Neurological Association at: www.aneuroa.org

Building and Construction

bridge engineering

comparison of insulation materials

comparison of strengths of building materials

effects of earthquakes on structures

effects of weather upon structures

fire preventative building materials

study of strains and stresses

For information and contacts on this subject, visit American Society of Civil Engineers at: www.asce.org

C

Carbohydrates

amounts needed in diet

effects on blood glucose levels

metabolism of

Cellular Phones/Wireless Technology

industrial applications of wireless technology

physiological effects on nonionizing radiation

study of cell phone usage and effect on driving ability

Chemistry

comparison of chemical bonds

effects of chemical reactions

effects of chemical toxins in the environment

effects on crystal growth

methods for absorbing wastewater metallic ions

use of atomic absorption spectroscopy

For information and contacts on this subject, visit American Chemical Society at: www.chemistry.org

Children

learning disorders in

methods for modifying behavior

sleeping needs of

study of childhood diseases

study of growth and development in children

Cigarettes

collection efficiency of cigarette filters

methods to assist others to stop smoking

physiological effects of firsthand smoke compared to secondhand smoke

For information and contacts on this subject, visit American Lung Association at: www.lungusa.org/tobacco

Color

color chromatography in various substances

effects of, on plant growth

perception of

psychological effects of

physiological effects of

Computers

developing various algorithms and code for

program designs for

robotic applications for

Corrosion

methods for the prevention of

role of microbes in

study of chemical changes in

For information and contacts on this subject, visit National Metalizing Association at: www.emetalizing.com

Crystals

applications of chemical crystallography

comparison of structures between various types

factors affecting the growth of

magnetic properties of

mathematical patterns found in

For information and contacts on this subject, visit American Crystallographic Association at: www.hwi.buffalo.edu/ACA

D

Dairy Studies

comparison of animal feeds

effects of dairy products on digestion

effects of hormone additive diets in cows

microbial action in dairy products

natural methods for preserving dairy products

treatment of viruses in dairy cattle

For information and contacts on this subject, visit American Dairy Science Association at: www.adsa.org

E

Environmental Studies

analysis of a closed ecological system or biosphere

analysis of biodegradable substances

effects of pollutants on wildlife

handling and transportation of toxic wastes

landfills and groundwater contamination

neutralization of toxic wastes

study of soil or water purification systems

For information and contacts on this subject, visit Environmental Protection Agency at: www.epa.gov

Erosion

effects of soil composition

effects of weather in

methods for controlling

For information and contacts on this subject, visit National Soil Erosion Research Laboratory at: www.topsoil. nserl.purdue.edu

Eye

color and light sensitivity of

effects of age on peripheral vision

effects of laser surgery upon

effects of ultraviolet radiation on

effects of various vitamin supplements

perception of optical illusions among age groups

study of abnormalities in

study of diseases in

For information and contacts on this subject, visit American Academy of Ophthalmology at: www.aao.org

F

Fermentation

analysis of enzymatic stimulation

applications of yeast in

identification and role of microbes in

study of chemical changes in

For information and contacts on this subject, visit American Society of Brewing Chemists at: www.asbcnet.org

Fertilizers

chemistry and composition of

comparison and evaluation of various types

comparison of organic and inorganic types

effects on the environment

For information and contacts on this subject, visit International Fertilizer Industry Association at: www.fertilizer.org

Fish

comparison of different species

effects of contaminated water on

medicinal uses of fish oils

migration patterns of

study of diseases found in

For information and contacts on this subject, visit American Society of Ichthyologists and Herpetologists at: http://199.245.200.110

Food

allergic reactions to

analysis and comparison of radiated food quality

body absorption of nutrients from

comparison of nutritional contents of

dehydration and preservation of

effects of packing on

effects of pesticides on food quality

food-dwelling microbes

methods of treating contamination of

physiological effects of additives used for preservation

For information and contacts on this subject, visit American Society of Agricultural Engineers at: www.asae.org

Fungi

environmental effects of mold spores

means for preventing the growth of

medicinal uses of

practical applications of for industry

G

Gasoline

analysis of the by-products from

chemistry and composition of

comparison of efficiency of various octane levels

For information and contacts on this subject, visit U.S. Department of Energy at: www.energy.gov

Genetics

genetic mapping in bacteria

methods for transferring genes

studies in plant cloning

study of genetic diseases

Geology

relationship between the moon and earthquake activity

study of earthquake activity

study of flood management and containment

study of the geologic history of an area

study of volcanic activity

For information and contacts on this subject, visit U.S. Geological Survey at: www.usgs.gov/index.html

Gerontology

correlation between mental activity and health in elders

effects on Alzheimer's disease

study of changes in the senses of the elderly

For information and contacts on this subject, visit American Geriatrics Society at: www.americangeriatrics.org

Glucose

metabolism in the body

study of sugar inversion

study of treatment of diabetes

For information and contacts on this subject, visit American Diabetes Association at: www.diabetes.org

H

Hair

effects of diet on

effects of disease on

hair transplanting techniques

physiological effects of hair dyes and chemicals

Health

analysis of various diets

analysis of various exercise programs

correlation between pH levels in hair products and hair quality

effects of climate on

side effects of medications

study of diseases and prevention thereof

For information and contacts on this subject, visit U.S. Department of Health and Human Services at: www.os.dhhs.gov

Heart

abnormalities in

effects of diet on

external effects on blood pressure and pulse rate

study of diseases found in

For information and contacts on this subject, visit American Heart Association at: www.americanheart.org

Heat

analysis of efficiency of various heating mechanisms

chemical reactions that produce heat

effects on chemical changes

insulation for retaining heat

therapeutic uses of

Hydraulics

analysis of turbines

methods for irrigation improvement

pumping design modifications

I

Ice

comparison of various ice melters

effects of, on bodily tissues

effects of, on microbes

therapeutic and surgical uses of

Immune System

in vitro immunization of cells

methods of vaccination

study of biochemical processes in

study of disorders affecting

For information and contacts on this subject, visit American Autoimmune Related Diseases Association at: www.aarda.org/index.html

Infants

chemistry and content of baby food/formula

presence of hand dexterity and preference in

study of growth and behavior of

Infrared Rays

effects of, on the environment

effects of, on heating

image converters

industrial applications of

therapeutic uses of

Insects

comparison of species in different locations

effects of diseases carried by

methods for extermination of

methods for sterilization of

parasitic effects of

study of behavior and communication in

For information and contacts on this subject, visit Entomological Society of America at: www.entsoc.org

L

Lasers

applications of lasers and optics

effects of, on the environment

uses of, in communications

uses of, in surgery

Learning

effects of diet on

effects of music on

memory, reasoning, and spatial abilities between age groups and gender types

methods for subliminal learning

study of learning disabilities

study of relationship between exercise and learning ability

Light

applications of, in photography

influence of, in chemical reactions

psychological effects of

therapeutic uses of

Lipids

amounts needed in diet

analysis of cholesterol tests

metabolism of

Liquids

comparison of surface tension between various liquids

effects of, on acoustics

viscosity comparisons

Lungs

effects of nutrition on

environmental effects on

study of diseases found in

For information and contacts on this subject, visit American Lung Association at: www.lungusa.org

M

Magnetics

effects of magnetic fields

industrial applications of magnets

medical uses of magnets

For information and contacts on this subject, visit International Magnetics Association at: www.intl-magnetics.org

Mathematics

analysis of various functions

correlation between number systems

mathematical patterning in music

mathematical patterning in nature

studies in probability

For information and contacts on this subject, visit American Mathematical Society at: www.ams.org

Metabolism

chemical factors affecting

effects of dieting on

effects of diet pills on

variation of, among animals

For information and contacts on this subject, visit American Association of Clinical Endocrinology at: www.aace.com

Metals

corrosion inhibitors

oxidation rate comparisons

refining processes

variations in the atomic densities of

For information and contacts on this subject, visit National Metalizing Association at: www.emetalizing.com

Meteorology

analysis of weather patterns

artificial effects upon weather

comparison of rainfall between locations

methods for forecasting

For information and contacts on this subject, visit American Meteorological Association at: www.ametsoc.org/AMS

Minerals

contents found in various soil samples

contents found in various water samples

medicinal uses of

as nutritional supplements

For information and contacts on this subject, visit American Mineralogical Society at: www.minsocam.org

Music

comparing sound quality between digital and analog recording

effects of music on learning

study of differences in tone quality between types of instruments

O

Ocean

effects of pollution on

methods for biodegrading oil spills

ocean waves as an energy source

For information and contacts on this subject, visit National Oceanic and Atmospheric Administration at: www.oar.noaa.gov

Oil

effects of, on the environment

methods for improving underwater drilling oil risers

nontraditional applications in industry

reclamation and recycling of oil

refining modifications

For information and contacts on this subject, visit American Petroleum Institute at: www.api-ec.api.org

Orthopedics

artificial joint designs

prosthetic device designs

study of therapeutic exercises

For information and contacts on this subject, visit American Academy of Orthopaedic Surgeons at: www.aaos.org

P

Parasites

methods for extermination of

prevention of parasitic microbes

study of parasitic diseases

For information and contacts on this subject, visit American Society of Parasitologists at: asp.unl.edu

Pesticides

biodegradation of

effects of, on health

effects of, on the environment

improving the effectiveness of

storage containers for

For information and contacts on this subject, visit Environmental Protection Agency at: www.epa.gov

Photography

effects of temperature on film

lens modifications

methods of surgical use of

uses of laser photography

Plastics

alternative industrial applications for

effects of, on the environment

effects of radiation on

modification of injection molding processes

recycling methods for

surgical applications of

For information and contacts on this subject, visit American Plastics Council at: www.americanplasticscouncil.org

Pollution

analysis of purification mechanisms

analysis of sewage disposal mechanisms

chemistry and composition of various water and soil samples

methods for controlling

For information and contacts on this subject, visit Environmental Protection Agency at: www.epa.gov

Ponds, Lakes, Rivers

analysis of seasonal changes in, on wildlife

analysis of water quality among locations

chemistry and composition of water samples

comparison of dissolved oxygen rates among locations

current power as an energy source

eutrophication in

methods for water purification

For information and contacts on this subject, visit Ecological Society of America at: www.esa.org

Proteins

lipoprotein patterns in various age groups

metabolism of, in various animals

nutritional importance of

study of protein synthesis

For information and contacts on this subject, visit The Protein Society at: www.faseb.org/protein

R

Radiation

effects of nonionizing radiation

methods of protection against

physiological effects of

uses of, in food preservation

uses of, in sterilization

Radiography/Radiology

industrial applications of

physiological side effects of

uses of, in medicine

For information and contacts on this subject, visit Radiological Society of North America at: www.rsna.org

Radios

comparison of power supplies for

electromagnetic emissions from

methods of eliminating radio interference

methods for improving sound in

radio frequency uses

For information and contacts on this subject, visit American Radio Relay League at: www.arrl.org

Rain/Precipitation

chemistry and composition of raindrops

comparison of rainfall patterns among
  locations

study of rain erosion

For information and contacts on this subject, visit American Meteorological Society at: www.ametsoc.org/ASM

Recycling

comparison of recycling techniques

effects of, on the internal bonding of
  paper

methods for recycling various materials

methods of developing a waste
  management system

For information and contacts on this subject, visit National Recycling Coalition at: www.nrc-recycle.org

S

Salt

antibacterial effects of

environmental effects of

physiological effects of

use in preservation

use of, as a fertilizer

Seawater

chemistry and composition of

effects of environment on

oil spill cleanup solutions

study of corrosion by

study of microbes from various ocean
  locations

Seeds

effects of radiation on

germination techniques

study of diseases in

Sewage

as an energy resource

chemistry and composition of

methods for the purification of

study of the biodegradation of

use of, as a fertilizer

Skin

effects of medication on

effects of ultraviolet radiation on

methods of protecting and improving
  quality of

methods of skin grafting

study of diseases found in

For information and contacts on this subject, visit American Academy of Dermatology at: www.aad.org

Sleep

effects of, on behavior

effects of sleep deprivation

influence of, on circadian rhythms

methods to stop snoring

observation of various stages of

physiological needs for in children and
  adults

study of sleeping disorders

For information and contacts on this subject, visit American Academy of Sleep Medicine at: www.aasmnet.org

Soil

effects of microbes on

chemistry and composition of

methods of conservation of

methods for controlling erosion of

Sun

comparison of solar energy with other
  sources

evaluation of lotions with various sun
  protection factors

measure of radiation from, at various
  locations and times

medicinal effects of

T

Telescopes

factors affecting resolution powers in

modifications of

study of various lenses

use of mathematics in

Tobacco

analysis of substitutes for

chemistry and composition of

diseases caused by

use of, as a fertilizer

U

Ultraviolet Rays

effects of, on plants/animals

therapeutic uses of

use of, for water purification

V

Vaccinations

methods of inoculating

physiological side effects of

serum sources

Vitamins/Nutraceuticals

study of deficiencies of

study of interaction between vitamins and
medication

study of metabolism of, in the human
body

therapeutic uses of

For information and contacts on this
subject, visit American Nutraceutical
Association at: www.americanutra.com

W

Water

analysis of water quality between various
locations

chemistry and composition of

comparison of pH levels between various
locations

effects of pollution on

methods of purification of

study of filtration methods

For information and contacts on this
subject, visit American Water Works
Association at: www.awwa.org

Wildlife

methods for improving habitats of

methods of conservation of

prevention of disease in

For information and contacts on this
subject, visit National Wildlife Federation
at: www.nwf.org

Wind

comparison of windmill designs

effects of, on soil erosion

study of wind turbines

use of, as an energy source

wind tunnel study

For information and contacts on this
subject, visit American Wind Energy
Association at: www.awea.org

Wood

chemistry and composition of various
types

fireproofing techniques

microbes found in

recycling techniques of

use of, as an energy source

For information and contacts on this
subject, visit American Forest and Paper
Association at: www.afandpa.org

Y

Yeast

chemistry and composition of

industrial uses of

physiological effects of

uses of, in fermentation

APPENDIX B

100+ PROJECT TITLES OF AWARD-WINNING PROJECTS

The following is a list of over one hundred actual science fair project titles taken from award-winning science fair projects at a variety of recent state and regional Intel ISEF–affiliated science fairs that may help generate some ideas for you. The topics are broken down by Intel ISEF categories of scientific discipline.

Behavioral and Social Science
Does Hearing a Type of Unfamiliar Music Frequently Increase One's Like or Dislike for It?

Does Color Affect the Way One Feels?

Does Subliminal Imaging Affect Decision Making?

Can Animals Instinctively Select Foods That Are Most Nutritionally Beneficial to Them through the Use of Their Senses?

Does Stress through Physical Exercise Affect One's Cognitive Ability?

Does Right or Left Handedness Affect Overall Lateral Dominance?

Do Behavioral Patterns of Smokers Affect Their Ability to Quit Smoking?

What Is the Best Time of Day for Students of Different Ages to Study?

Does One's Perception of Elapsed Time Vary When They Are Working versus Not Working?

Does a Correlation Exist between Sensory Arousal and the Mozart Effect?

The Relationship between Obsessive-Compulsive Disorder and Birth Order

Biochemistry
The Effects of Glucose on Cell Volume

Does the Percentage of Reduced Fat in Food Correspond to the Same Percentage Change in Calories?

Which Brand of Plastic Zipper Bags Keeps Bread Fresher Longer?

What Are the Effects of Various Cooking Methods on the Depletion of Vitamin C?

A Comparison of the Durability of Latent Fingerprints Using Cyanoacrylate and Nonpreserved Latent Fingerprints

Can Calorie Restriction Enhance the Ability of Cells to Survive DNA-Damaging UV Light Exposure?

The Effects of Various Preservatives on the Spoilage of Milk

The Effect of Antacids on E. Coli Found in Hamburger Meat in the Presence of Gastric Fluid

Botany
Plant Growth under Different Wavelengths of Light

Which Plant Food Works the Best?

The Effect of Water Temperature on Various Species of Phytoplankton

The Effects of the Use of Antagonistic Microorganisms in Controlling Fruit Rot

If Music Affects Plant Growth, What Type of Music Has the Most Impact?

Does Altering the Gravity of Bean Plants Affect Their Growth?

Does the Increase of Oxygen Concentration Enhance the Germination Rate of Plant Seeds?

Does Water Type Affect the Height of Grass?

The Effects of Mature Leaf Position on Stomatal Development in New Leaves in Response to Carbon Dioxide Levels

How Does Radiation Affect the Growth and Germination of Radish Seeds?

What Type of Animal Manure Will Have the Most Positive Growth Effect on Plants?

Can Wheat Gluten Be Used as a Natural Preemergent Herbicide Like Corn Gluten Meal?

Which Filamentous Algae Can Recycle Carbon Dioxide into Oxygen Most Efficently?

Which Variable, Namely, Species Type, Tree Size, or Seed Mass Has the Most Effect on the Ability of a Maple Tree to Reproduce?

Chemistry

Does Prewatering Soil Significantly Reduce Runoff during Normal Rainfall?

Does pH in the Intestine Affect the Absorption of Calcium in the Body?

Does Temperature Affect Battery Life?

The Effects of Light Intensity and Temperature on the Rate of the Photochemical Reaction of Silver Chloride

Does the Electrolytic Rates of Different Beverages Affect the Rate at Which the Body Receives Energy from the Beverage?

The Effect of Temperature on Surface Tension Strength

Which Type of Juice Beverage Is the Most Effective Means for Delivering Vitamin C to the Human Body?

Which Papier-mâché Adhesive Ingredient Is the Strongest?

Which Brand of Paint Preserves the Tensile Strength of Steel?

How Do Different Solutions Affect the Carbon Dioxide Production of Leavening Agents?

How Do Different Types of Water Affect the Rusting Process of Various Metals?

Does Cooking Acidic Foods in Aluminum Cookware Cause Traces of Aluminum to Leach into the Food?

What Substance Could Be Applied to Pretreat Airplane Wings to Aid in the Rapid Removal of Ice?

A Comparison of the Thermal Transport Properties of Water and Ethylene Glycol

Does Molarity Affect the Amount of Crystals Formed in the Electrolysis of Copper Sulfate, Aluminum Nitrate, and Iron Sulfate?

Does the Introduction of Protein Affect the Growth of the Crystalline Structural Lattice in Sodium Chloride?

Computer Science

Optimal Configuration of School Bus Routes Using the Computer Based Algorithm— Simulated Annealing

Can a Computer Learn Game Strategy by Analyzing Results over a Period of Time

Can Enlarged Images Be Depixelized?

Earth and Space Science

Are There Jet Stream Patterns That Affect Tornado Formation and Location?

The Effect of Gravity on Stress Response in Plants

Analysis of Soil Types for Strength

Effects of Soils and Surfaces on Water Runoff and Flooding

The Effects of Earthquakes on Small Structures

What Is the Structure to Prevent Beach Erosion?

What Shape of a Solar Reflector Reflects the Most Light into a Solar Cell?

The Effects of Fin Configuration on the Performance of a Model Rocket

Do Soils Change the Composition of Water?

Engineering

What Is the Best Type of Guardrail for an Inclining Mountain Road?

Is It Possible to Give a Prosthetic Limb Device the Ability to Be Felt by the Nerves of a Patient

Testing the Efficacy of Chest Protectors from Ball or Hockey Puck Impact

Can a Temporary Wheelchair Lift Be Constructed That Will Not Obstruct Stairs or Require Modifications to Existing Staircase Structures?

Environmental Science

What Glass Color Blocks Ultraviolet Rays the Best?

The Effects of Soil on Home Insulation

The Effects of Marine Paint on Sea Life

The Effect of Respirable Particles from Radial Tire Wear on Human Lungs

Environmental Effects of Biodegradable Detergents

A Chemical Investigation and Analysis of Ground and Surface Water in a Local Water Supply

The Effect of Water Hardness on Toxicity

Phototoxicity of Botanical Compounds to Insects and Yeast

The Effects of Radon in Water

Effects of Fertilization of Golf Courses on Drinking Water

Does Temperature Affect Solar Cell Performance?

Does the Distance That Water Travels from a Water Plant Affect the Amount of Lead in the Drinking Water?

Can Citrus Oils Be Used As a Substitute for Gasoline?

Are There Adequate Amounts of Carbon and Nitrogen in Soil after a Forest Fire to Affect Plant Growth?

Can Earthworms Decontaminate Soil Contaminated with Lead?

The Effects of Sugar, Coffee Pulp, and Alcohol on the Rate That *Eisenia foetida* Can Decompose Garbage

Gerontology

Does Age Affect One's Sense of Smell or Taste?

The Physiologic Effect of a Vegetarian Diet on the Elderly

The Effects of the Herb *Succus cineraria* Martima on the Size Distribution of Cataract Proteins

Health Science

The Effects of Air Pressure on Blood Clots

Can Antisense Genes Reverse Antibiotic Resistance?

The Long-term Effects of Antibacterial Soap on Normal Skin Flora

What Is the Effect of Varying Levels of pH on *Eschericia coli?*

Which Whitening Agents Whiten Teeth Best?

Do Colored Contact Lenses Affect Peripheral Vision?

How Effective Is Sunscreen Against Ultraviolet Light?

The Effect of Light on the Development of Rat Mammary Glands

Does the Addition of Fibroblast Growth Factor (FGF) Retard the Cancerous Growth of Tumors in Rats?

Which Antacid Will Neutralize the Most Stomach Acid?

The Effects of Nicotine on Angiogenesis-related Processes and Its Impact on Tumor Growth

Which Acne-Fighting Agent—Salicylic Acid, Benzoyl Peroxide, or Sulfur—works Best at Eradicating *Staphylococcus epidermis?*

Is There a Direct Relationship between Body Mass Index and Blood Pressure in Teenagers?

Mathematics

The Relationship between the Golden Ratio and Facial Perception

Is the Distribution of Differences between Prime Numbers Predictable or Chaotic?

Is There a Statistical Advantage to Winning in Baseball for the Team That Scores First in the Game?

Microbiology

The Effect of Ultraviolet Radiation on the Growth of Bacteria on Meat

Can Bacteria Become Resistant to Antibacterial Products Containing Triclosan, an Antibacterial Agent?

Do Synthetic or Nonsynthetic Emulsifiers Break Down Fat the Best?

The Effects of Preservatives in Bread and the Rate of Mold Growth

Can an Antibiotic-Resistant Bacteria Be Changed into an Antibiotic-Sensitive Bacteria?

The Effect of Phosphates on the Luminescence of Aerobic Marine Light-Emitting Bacteria

What Are the Effects of Atrazine, an Herbicide, on Bacterial Survival?

Do Biofilms Grow on Contact Lenses?

Can Bacteria Found on the Hands Become Resistant to Antibacterial Liquid Hand Soap?

Physics

Does the Frequency and Amplitude of Sound Waves from a Violin Change in Different Temperatures?

Can Sound Be Transmitted through a Laser Beam?

Does String Tension Affect the Rate at How Quickly a Tennis Racket's Strings Break?

The Effect of Balde Angle and Barometric Pressure on the Rotation Speed of a Windmill

Is There a Difference in Tone Quality between Plastic and Wooden Clarinets?

How Do Sound Waves Behave When Traveling through Carbon Dioxide?

What Type of Flooring Has the Strongest Sound Vibrations?

Which Type of Shoe Insert Absorbs the Most Shock on Impact?

What Is the Relationship between Barrier Thickness and the Percentage of Light That Tunnels through a Barrier?

What Properties of a Truss Affect Its Displacement?

How Does Shape Affect the Drag of an Object?

A Study of Heat Absorption and Dispersion on Various Colors of Metallic Paint

Zoology

The Effects of Citronella Oil, Peppermint Oil, and Teatree Oil As a Natural Pesticide on the Eradication of Mosquitos

Which Types of Soils Do Worms Prefer?

The Effects of Electromagnetic Fields on the Development and Behavior of Caterpillars

Is There a Relationship between the Number of Days It Takes Fruit Fly Eggs to Hatch and the Amount of Light They Are Exposed To?

Does Water Temperature Affect the Hatch Rate of Mosquitoes?

Does the Amount of Light Exposure Affect the Response of Euglena Populations to Acidic Polutants?

APPENDIX C

SCIENTIFIC SUPPLY COMPANIES

The following is a list of over twenty-five scientific supply companies from whom laboratory and other scientific supplies and instruments can be obtained. The companies were selected because they specialize in equipment geared to science fair projects or equipment that is normally used in a school laboratory.

Northeast and Atlantic

Auspex Scientific
1416 Union Boulevard
Allentown, PA 18109
(610) 351-2079
www.auspexscientific.com

Connecticut Valley Biological
    Supply Co.
82 Valley Rd.
P.O. Box 326
Southampton, MA 01703
(413) 527-4030
(800) 628-7748
www.ctvalleybio.com

Edmund Scientific Co.
60 Pearce Ave.
Tonawanda, NY 14150-6711
(800) 728-6999
www.scientificsonline.com

MiniScience.Com
1059 Main Ave.
Clifton, NJ 07011
(973) 777-3133
www.miniscience.com

The Science Fair, Inc.
140 College Square
Newark, DE 19711-5447
(302) 453-1817
(800) 304-9403
www.thesciencefair.com

Science Kit and Boreal Labs
777 E. Park Dr.
P.O. Box 5003
Tonawanda, NY 14150
(800) 828-7777
www.sciencekit.com

Thomas Scientific
P.O. Box 99
Swedesboro, NJ 08085
(856) 467-3087
(800) 345-5232
www.thomassci.com

Ward's Natural Science
P.O. Box 92912
Rochester, NY 14692-9012
(800) 962-2660
www.wardsci.com

Southeast

Advance Scientific & Chemical, Inc.
2345 S.W. 34th St.
Fort Lauderdale, FL 33312
(800) 524-2436
www.advance-scientific.com

Carolina Biological Supply Co.
2700 York Rd.
Burlington, NC 27215
(800) 334-5551
www.carolina.com

Kenin Scientific Discount
1830 N.E. 163 St.
North Miami Beach, FL 33162
(800) 600-6291
www.kenin.com

Science Hobbies, Inc.
901-D North Wendover Road
Charlotte, NC 28211
(704) 367-2215
www.sciencehobbies.net

Midwest

American Science & Surplus
5316 N. Milwaukee Ave.
Chicago, IL
(847) 647-0011
www.sciplus.com

BME Lab Store
2459 University Ave., W.
St. Paul, MN 55114
(651) 646-5339

Fisher Science Education
4500 Turnberry
Hanover Park, IL 60133
(800) 955-1177
www.fisheredu.com

Frey Scientific Co.
100 Paragon Parkway
Manfield, OH 44905
(800) 225-3739
www.freyscientific.com

Sargent-Welch
7300 N. Linden Ave.
P.O. Box 5229
Buffalo Grove, IL 60089-5229
(800) 727-4368
www.sargentwelch.com

South Central

Capitol Scientific, Inc.
2500 Rutland St.
Austin, TX 78766
(512) 836-1167

NASCO
901 Janesville Ave.
Fort Atkinson, WI 53538
(800) 558-9595
www.enasco.com

Sciencelab.com
4338 Haven Glen
Kingwood, TX 77339
(281) 348-9500
www.sciencelab.com

Science Stuff
1104 Newport Ave.
Austin, TX 78753-4019
(800) 795-7315
www.sciencestuff.com

West

All World Scientific
5515 186 Place SW
Lynnwood, WA 98037
425 672 4228
800- 28-WORLD
www.awscientific.com

Amico Scientific
1161 Cushman Ave.
San Diego, CA 92110
(619) 543-9200

A. Warren's Educational Supplies
980 W. San Bernardino Road
Covina, CA 91722
(800) 523-7767
www.warrenseducational.com

Hawaii Chemical & Scientific
2364 North King St.
Honolulu, HI 96811
(808) 841-4265
www.hawaiiscientific.com

Tri-Ess Sciences
1020 Chestnut St.
Burbank, CA 91506
(818) 848-7838
800-274-6910 (outside California)
www.tri-esssciences.com

Canada

Northwest Scientific Supply
P.O. Box 6100 # 301-3060
Cedar Hill Road
VICTORIA, BC
V8T 3J5
CANADA
(250) 592-2438
www.nwscience.com

APPENDIX D

STATE, REGIONAL, AND INTERNATIONAL SCIENCE AND ENGINEERING FAIRS

There are many wonderful science and engineering fairs throughout the United States and around the world. Since many of these fairs change administrators or names yearly, it is impossible to list all of them. Therefore, this list contains the name of state, regional, and international science and engineering fairs that are currently charter affiliated with the Intel International Science and Engineering Fair. These fairs are held annually on various dates from February through May. While these fairs play host to thousands of top science fair exhibits from students in grades 6–12, only students in grades 9–12 from these fairs are eligible to participate in the annual Intel International Science and Engineering Fair, which is administered by Science Service, Inc.

The following is a list of all affiliated fairs and their hosting cities along with their corresponding website addresses, if available. We have listed websites that have been online for awhile so we hope they will still be around by the time you read this. The names, addresses and telephone numbers of fair administrators, as well as the specific dates of these fairs, have not been included because they often change on a yearly basis. However, if you would like to obtain specific information about any of the listed fairs, contact Science Service, Inc., 1719 N. Street, N.W., Washington, D.C. 20036. Telephone (202) 785-2255.

United States

Alabama

Livingston: West Alabama Science and Engineering Fair
(205) 652-3414

Alaska

Juneau: Southeast Alaska Regional Science Fair
www.asd.k12.ak.us/Depts/Science/ sciencefair/sciencefair.htm

Arizona

Prescott: Northern Arizona Regional Science and Engineering Fair
http://sciencefair.pr.erau.edu

Sierra Vista: SSVEC's Youth Engineering and Science Fair
http://ssvec.org/CommunityPrograms/ yesfair.asp

Tempe: Central Arizona Regional Science and Engineering Fair
www.carsef.asu.edu

Tucson: Southern Arizona Regional
Science and Engineering Fair
www.sarsef.com

Arkansas

Batesville: North Central Arkansas
Regional Science Fair
www.lyon.edu

Conway: Arkansas State Science Fair

Fayetteville: Northwest Arkansas
Regional Science Science and
Engineering Fair
www.uark.edu/~k12info

Hot Springs: West Central Regional
Science Fair

Jonesboro: Northeast Arkansas Regional
Science Fair
http://nearsf.astate.edu

Monticello: Southeast Arkansas Regional
Science Fair

California

Carson: South Bay Regional Science &
Engineering Fair

Danville: Tri-Valley Science and
Engineering Fair
http://tvsef.llnl.gov

Sacramento: Sacramento Regional
Science & Engineering Fair
www.srsefair.org

San Diego: Greater San Diego Science
and Engineering Fair
www.gsdsef.org

San Francisco: San Francisco Bay Area
Science Fair, Inc.
http://home.pacbell.net/sfbasf/

San Jose: Synopsys Silicon Valley Science
and Technology Championship
www.science-fair.org

Santa Cruz: Santa Cruz County Science
Fair
www.science.santacruz.k12.ca.us

Seaside: Monterey County Science and
Engineering Fair
www.nps.navy.mil/mcsfp/

Colorado

Alamosa: San Luis Valley Regional
Science Fair, Inc.
http://slv.adams.edu/science/index.htm

Boulder: Boulder Valley Regional Science
Fair

Colorado Springs: Pikes Peak Regional
Science Fair

Denver: The Denver Metro Regional
Science & Engineering Fair
www.uchsc.edu/ahec/sciencefair/
index.htm

Fort Collins: Colorado Science and
Engineering Fair
www.csef.colostate.edu

Grand Junction: Western Colorado
Science Fair

Greeley: Longs Peak Science and
Engineering Fair
http://hopper.unco.edu/Other/
Sciencefair.html

La Junta: Arkansas Valley Regional
Science Fair

San Juan Basin Regional Science Fair
http://faculty.fortlewis.edu/
IVERSON_M/sciencefair.htm

Sterling: Northeast Colorado Regional
Science Fair

Connecticut

Hamden: Connecticut State Science Fair
http://ctsciencefair.org

New Milford: Science Horizons Science
Fair & Symposium
www.sciencehorizons.org

Florida

Arcadia: Heartland Regional Science and
Engineering Fair

Bradenton: Manatee Regional Science
and Engineering Fair

Bushnell: Sumter County Regional
Science Fair

Crystal River: Citrus Regional Science
and Engineering Fair

Fort Myers: Thomas Alva Edison East Regional Science Fair

Fort Pierce: Treasure Coast Regional Science and Engineering Fair

Kissimmee: The Osceola Regional Science Fair

Melbourne: South Brevard Science and Engineering Fair

Merritt Island: Brevard Intracoastal Regional Science and Engineering Fair

Miami: South Florida Science and Egineering Fair
http://mathscience.dadeschools.net/sciencefair.htm

Ocala: Big Springs Regional Science Fair

Orange Park: Clay Kiwanis Science Fair

Panama City: Florida Three Rivers Regional Science and Engineering Fair

Pinellas Park: Pinellas Regional Science and Engineering Fair

Sanford: Seminole County Regional Science, Mathematics & Engineering Fair

Sarasota: Sarasota Regional Science, Engineering and Technology Fair
www.sarasota.k12.fl.us/brookside/aoft/at6/science/science%5Ffair.htm

Titusville: Brevard Mainland Regional Science and Engineering Fair

Wesley Chapel: PASCO Regional Science and Engineering Fair

West Palm Beach: Palm Beach County Science and Engineering Fair

Georgia

Albany: Darton College/Merck Regional Science Fair

Athens: Georgia State Science and Engineering Fair
www.uga.edu/oasp/gsef/gsef.html

Atlanta: Atlanta Science and Mathematics Congress
http://1sblackburn@atlantak12.ga.us

Atlanta: The Earthlink Dekalb-Rockdale Science & Engineering Fair

Augusta: CSRA Regional Science & Engineering Fair
http://csrascience.org

Brunswick: Coastal Georgia Regional Science and Engineering Fair

Savannah: Savannah Ogeechee Regional Science and Engineering Fair

Warner Robins: Houston Regional Science and Engineering Fair

Hawaii

Honolulu: Hawaii State Science and Engineering Fair
www.hawaii.edu/acadsci

Kahului: Maui Schools Science and Technology Fair

Kapaa: Kauai Regional Science & Engineering Fair

Pearl City: Leeward District High School Science Fair

Illinois

Macomb: Heart of Illinois Science and Engineering Fair

Indiana

Angola: Northeastern Indiana Tri-State Regional Science Fair

Evansville: Tri-State Regional Science and Engineering Fair

Fort Wayne: Northeastern Indiana Reginal Science and Engineering Fair
http://ipfw.edu/scifair

Muncie: East Central Indiana Regional Science Fair

South Bend: Northern Indiana Regional Science and Engineering Fair

Westville: Northwestern Indiana Science and Engineering Fair
www.purduenc.edu/cd/scifair.index.html

Iowa

Ames: State Science and Engineering
Fair of Iowa
www.public.iastate.edu/~isstf/

Cedar Rapids: Eastern Iowa Science and
Engineering Fair
www.eisef.org

Indianola: South Central Iowa Science
and Engineering Fair

Kansas

Overland Park: Greater Kansas City
Science and Engineering Fair
http://spioneers.com

Kentucky

Bowling Green: Southern Kentucky
Regional Science Fair

Owensboro: Owensboro-Western
Kentucky Regional Fair

Louisiana

Baton Rouge: Louisiana Science and
Engineering Fair
www.doce.lsu.edu/lsef/

Houma: Terrebonne Parish Science Fair

Lafayette: Louisiana Region VI Science
and Engineering Fair

Lake Charles: Louisiana Region V
Science and Engineering Fair
www.lasciencefair.org

Thibodaux: Louisiana Region X Science
and Engineering Fair

Maryland

Baltimore: Morgan State University

Science-Mathematics-Engineering Fair

Frederick: Frederick County Science
and Engineering Fair

Gaithersburg: Mongomery Area Science
Fair

Laplata: Charles County Science Fair

Largo: Prince George's Area Science
Fair
http://users.erols.com/gorthome/
hpsfmain.htm

Massachusetts

Amherst: Massachusetts Region I
Science Fair
www.scifair.com

Boston: Massachusetts Region VI
Science Fair
www.scifair.com

Bridgewater: Massachusetts Region V
Science Fair
www.scifair.com

Cambridge: Massachusetts State
Science Fair
www.scifair.com

Fall River: Massachusetts Region III
Science Fair
www.scifair.com

Somerville: Massachusetts Region IV
Science Fair
www.scifair.com

Worcester: Massachusetts Region II
State Science Fair
www.scifair.com

Michigan

Ann Arbor: Southeast Michigan Science
Fair

Detroit: Science and Engineering Fair of
Metropolitan Detroit
www.sefmd.org

Flint: Flint Area Science Fair
www.flintsciencefair.org

Port Huron: St. Clair County Science and
Engineering Fair

Minnesota

Duluth: Northeast Minnesota Regional
Science Fair
www.css.edu/USERS/lmcgahey/
web/RegionalSF/main.html

Mankato: South Central/South
Minnesota Regional Science and
Engineering Fair
www.mnsu.edu/sciencefair

Minneapolis: Minnesota Academy of
Science State Fair
www.mnacadsci.org

Minneapolis: Twin Cities Regional
Science Fair
www.tcrsf.org

Moorhead: Western Minnesota Regional
Science Fair

Rochester: Rochester Regional Science
Fair

Saint Cloud: Central Minnesota Regional
Science Fair and Research paper
Program

Winona: Southeast Minnesota Regional
Science Fair

Mississippi

Booneville: Mississippi Region IV
Science Fair

Greenville: Mississippi Region III
Science and Engineering
Fair

Hattiesburg: University of Southern
Mississippi Region I Science and
Engineering Fair

Oxford: Mississippi VII Science and
Engineering Fair
www.outreach.olemiss.edu/youth/
science_fair.html

Missouri

Cape Girardeau: Southeast Missouri
Regional Science Fair
www2.semo.edu/scifair/general.pdf

Jefferson City: Lincoln University
Regional Science Fair

Joplin: Missouri Southern Regional
Science Fair
www.mssc.edu/isef

Saint Joseph: Mid-America Regional
Science and Engineering Fair

Springfield: Ozarks Science and
Engineering Fair
www.k12science.smsu.edu

St. Peters: St. Charles-Lincoln Country
Regional Science and Engineering
Fair

Montana

Billings: Deaconess Billings Clinic
Research Division Science Expo
http://billingsclinic.com/Research/
ScienceExpo.htm

Butte: Southwest Montana Regional
Science and Engineering Fair
http://mtech.edu/outreach/
sciencefair.htm

Missoula: Montana Science Fair
http://hawk.cs.umt.edu/scifair

Nebraska

Greater Nebraska Science and
Engineering Fair
www.gnsef.org

Nevada

Elko: Elko County Science Fair

Reno: Western Nevada Regional Science
and Engineering Fair

New Jersey

Lawrenceville: Mercer Science and
Engineering Fair

North Branch: North Jersey Regional
Science Fair
http://njrsf.org

New Mexico

Albuquerque: Northwestern New
Mexico Regional Science and
Engineering Fair
www.unm.edu/~scifair

Albuquerque: National American Indian
Science and Engineering Fair
www.aises.org

Farmington: San Juan New Mexico
Regional Science and Engineering
Fair

Las Cruces: Southwestern New Mexico
Regional Science and Engineering
Fair
www.nmsu.edu/~scifair/

Las Vegas: Northeastern New Mexico
Regional Science and Engineering
Fair
www.nmhu.edu/sciencefair/

New York

Brooklyn: Polytechnic University and NYC Board of Education Math, Science, and Technology Fair

Long Island: Long Island Science and Engineering Fair
www.lisef.org

Plainview: New York State Science & Engineering Fair
www.NYSSEF.org

Poughkeepsie: Dutchess County Regional Science Fair

Rochester: Central Western Section—Science Teachers Association of NY State Science Congress

Syracuse: Greater Syracuse Scholastic Science Fair
http://most.org/p_gsssf_main.cfm

Troy: Greater Capital Region Science and Engineering Fair

Utica: Utica College Regional Science Fair

Westchester: Progenics Westchester Science and Engineering Fair
www.wesef.org

North Dakota

Dickinson: Southwest North Dakota Regional Science and Engineering Fair

Fargo: Southeast North Dakota Regional Science and Engineering Fair

Grand Forks: Northeast North Dakota Regional Science and Engineering Fair

Jamestown: Southeast Central North Dakota Science and Engineering Fair

Minot: Northwest Central North Dakota Regional Science Fair

Watford City: Northwest North Dakota Regional Science Fair

Ohio

Alliance: Ohio Region XIII Science and Engineering Fair

Archbold: Northwest Ohio Science and Engineering Fair

Athens: Southeastern Ohio Regional Science and Engineering Fair
www.ohiou.edu/scifair/

Cleveland: Northeastern Ohio Science and Engineering Fair
neohioscifair.org

Columbus: Buckeye Science and Engineering Fair
www.ohiosci.org

Marion: Marion Area Science and Engineering Fair

Shaker Heights: Hathaway Brown Upper School

Wilberforce: Miami Valley Science and Engineering Fair

Oklahoma

Ada: Oklahoma State Science and Engineering Fair
http://ecok.edu/ossef

Alva: Northwestern Oklahoma State University Regional Science Fair

Edmond: Central Oklahoma Regional Science and Engineering Fair
http://science.ucok.edu/science-fair.html

Miami: Northeastern Oklahoma A&M Science and Engineering Fair
www.neoam.cc.ok.us/sef

Muskogee: Muskogee Regional Science and Engineering Fair

Oklahoma City: Oklahoma City Regional Science and Engineering Fair

Seminole: East Central Oklahoma Regional Science and Engineering Fair

Tulsa: Tulsa Regional Science and Engineering Fair

Wilburton: Eastern Oklahoma Regional Science and Engineering Fair

Oregon

Beaverton: Beaverton School District Science Expo

Coos Bay: Southwestern Oregon Regional Science Exposition

Portland: Intel Northwest Science Expo
www.cse.pdx.edu/nwse

West Linn: CREST- Jane Goodall Science Symposium

Pennsylvania

Carlisle: The Patriot-News Capital Area Science and Engineering Fair

Lancaster: Lancaster Newspapers Science and Engineering Fair
www.lancasteronline.com/nie/scifair.shtm

Philadelphia: Delaware Valley Science Fair
www.dvsf.org

Pittsburgh: Pittsburgh Regional Science and Engineering Fair
www.pittsburghsciencefair.org

Reading: Reading and Berks Science and Engineering Fair

Rhode Island

Warwick: Rhode Island Science and Engineering Fair

South Carolina

Aiken: Central Savannah River Area Science and Engineering Fair
www.csrascience.org

Charleston: Lowcountry Science Fair

Clemson: Anderson-Oconee-Pickens Regional Science Fair
www.ces.clemson.edu/aophub/sciencefair

Columbia: USC Central South Carolina Region II Science and Engineering Fair

Greensville: Greensville County & South Regional 1A Science and Engineering Fair

Spartanburg: Piedmont South Carolina Region III Science Fair

South Dakota

Aberdeen: Northern South Dakota Science and Math Fair

Brookings: Eastern South Dakota Science and Engineering Fair
ww3.sdstate.edu/Academics/ScienceandEngineeringFair/Index.cfm

Isabel: Northwest Area Schools Regional Science and Engineering Fair

Mitchell: South Central South Dakota Science and Engineering Fair
www.dwusciencefair.com

Rapid City: High Plains Regional Science and Engineering Fair
www.hpcnet.org/science

Tennessee

Chattanooga: Chattanooga Regional Science and Engineering Fair

Cookeville: Cumberland Plateau Regional Science and Engineering Fair
www.tntech.edu/physics

Knoxville: Southern Appalachian Science and Engineering Fair
www.acad.utk.edu/sasef

Memphis: Memphis-Shelby County Science and Engineering Fair

Nashville: Middle Tennessee Science and Engineering Fair
www.vuse.vanderbilt.edu/~scifair/intro.html

Texas

Arlington: Exxon Mobil Texas Science and Engineering Fair
science.uta.edu/emtsef

Austin: Austin Area Science Festival
www.sciencefest.austinenergy.com

Brownsville: Rio Grande Valley Regional Science and Engineering Fair

College Station: Brazos Valley Regional Science and Engineering Fair
http://outreach.science.tamu.edu

Dallas: Dallas Morning News— Toyota Reg. Science and Engineering Fair
http://DallasScienceFair.org

El Paso: Sun Country Science Fair

Forth Worth: Forth Worth Regional
Science Fair
www.fwrsf.org

Houston: Science Engineering Fair of
Houston
http://uhd.edu/naturalscience

Kilgore: East Texas Regional Science
Fair

Laredo: United Independent School
District Regional Science Fair
www.uisd.net

San Angelo: District XI Texas Science
Fair

San Antonio: Alamo Regional Science
and Engineering Fair

Waco: Central Texas Science and
Engineering Fair
http://ctsef.org

Utah

Cedar City: Utah Science and
Engineering Fair

Ogden: Ogden Area I Science and
Engineering Fair

Ogden: Harold W. & Helen M. Ritchey
State Science and Engineering Fair of
Utah

Provo: Central Utah Science and
Engineering Fair
www.cusef.byu.edu

Salt Lake City: Salt Lake City Valley
Regional Science & Engineering
Fair
www.utah.edu/uees/fair

Virginia

Arlington: Northern Virginia Science
and Engineering Fair

Ashburn: Loudoun County Regional
Science and Engineering Fair

Ashland: Virginia State Science and
Engineering Fair

Charlottesville: Piedmont Regional
Science Fair

Dublin: Blue Ridge Highlands Regional
Science Fair

Fairfax: Fairfax County Regional Science
and Engineering Fair
www.fcps.edu/dis/sciengfair

Harrisonburg: Shenandoah Valley
Regional Science Fair

Lynchburg: Central Virginia Regional
Science Fair
www.cvgs.k12.va.us/scifair

Manassas: Prince William-Manassas
Regional Science Fair

Roanoke: Western Virginia Regional
Science Fair

Suffolk: Tidewater Science Fair
www.sps.k12.va.us

Washington

Kennwick: Mid-Columbia Regional
Science and Engineering Fair
www.mcsf.net

Tacoma: South Sound Regional Science
Fair
www.plu.edu/~scifair

West Virginia

Huntington: West Virginia State Science
and Engineering Fair
www.wvssef.org

Keyser: West Virginia Eastern
Panhandle Regional High School
Science Fair

Montgomery: Central and Southern
West Virginia Regional Science and
Engineering Fair
www.wvutech.edu/sciencefair

Wisconsin

Glendale: Nicolet Science and
Engineering Fair

Milwaukee: USM—Science Fair

Wyoming

Greybull: Northern Wyoming
District Science Fair

Outside the United States
American Samoa

Pago Pago: American Samoa Science Fair

Australia

Sydney: Intel Young Scientist Awards
www.stansw.asn.au

Belarus

Minsk: BelJunior
www.unibel.by

Brazil

Novo Hamburgo: National Science and
Technology Fair
http://liberato.com.br

San Paulo: Febrace – Feira Brasileira de
Ciencias E Engenharia-Regional Sao
Paulo

Canada

Hamilton, Ontario: Bay Area Science and
Engineering Fair
http://basef.mcmaster.ca

Montreal, Quebec: Montreal Regional
SciTech Fair
www.eascitech.org

China

Beijing: Children Science Fair of Beijing

Beijing: CASTIC (China Adolescents and
Technology Invention Contest)

Fuzhou City: CASTIC (China
Adolescents and Technology
Invention Contest)

Hefei City: CASTIC (China Adolescents
and Technology Invention Contest)

Hong Kong: Hong Kong Youth Science
and Technology Invention Contest
www.newgen.org.hk

Shanghai: CASTIC (China Adolescents
and Technology Invention Contest)

Shanghai: The Children Science Fair of
Shanghai

Czech Republic

Holesov: Students' Professional
Activities (SPA)

Denmark

Copenhagen: Unge Forskere

Germany

Stuttgart and Jena
www.jugend-forscht.de

Hungary

Budapest: Innovation Contest for Young
Scientists
www.innovacio.hu

India

Mumbai: Intel Science Talent Discovery
Fair—West

New Delhi: Intel Science Talent
Discovery Fair—North

Ireland

Dublin: EAST BT Young Scientist &
Technology Exhibition
www.esatbtyoungscientist.com

Israel

Jerusalem: Young Scientists in Israel—
Contest
www.mada.org.il

Italy

Milano: Giovani E Le Scienze
www.fast.mi.it

Japan

Tokyo: Japan Students Science Awards

Kazakhsta

Astana: DARYN National Junior Science
Projects Competition

Northern Ireland

Belfast: Seagate Young Innovators

Norway

Oslo: Norwegian Contest for Young
Scientists
www.unge-forskere.no/stiftelsen

Philippines

Manila: Intel Basic Philippine Science
Fair

Manila: Intel Philippine Applied Science
Fair

Portugal

Porto: Portuguese Contest for Young Scientists
www.fjuventude.pt

Puerto Rico

Arecibo: Arecibo Regional Science Fair

Bayamon: Bayamon Regional Science Fair

Caguas: Caguas Regional Science Fair

Cayey: Radians Science & Engineering Fair

Fajardo: Fajardo Regional Science Fair

Guaynabo: San Juan Archdiocesan Regional Science Fair

Gurabo: Humacao Regional Science Fair

Manati: Morovis Regional Science Fair

Mayaguez: Mayaguez Regional Science Fair

Ponce: Ponce Regional Science Fair

San German: San German Regional Scinece Fair

San Juan: Regional Mathematics Fair

San Juan: San Juan Regional Science Fair

Russia

Lipetsk: Russian Youth Program "Step into the Future"

Moscow: Russian Youth Program "Step into the Future"
www.apfn.bmstu.ru

Moscow: Intel-Avangard
www.1303.ru

Murmansk: Russian Youth Program "Step into the Future"

Snezhinsk: Russian Youth Program "Step into the Future"

Usolye-Sibirskoye: Russian Youth Program "Step into the Future"
www.shag-irkutsk.nm.ru

South Africa

Pretoria: Expo for Young Scientists— South Africa
www.exposcience.co.za

South Korea

Seoul: Korea Olympiad in Informatics

Sweden

Stockholm: Utstallningen Unga Forskare
www.fuf.org

Taiwan

Taipei: National Science and Engineering Fair of Republic of China
www.ntsec.gov.tw

Thailand

Bangkok: National Science Projects Competition
www.scisoc.or.th

United Kingdom

London: The BA Science Fair
www.the-ba.net

Virgin Islands

St. Croix: Good Hope School Science Fair

APPENDIX E

ALTERNATIVE SCIENCE FAIR PROJECT COMPETITIONS

This book emphasizes the preparation of science projects for traditional science fair competitions. These fairs are usually state and regional competitions affiliated with the Intel International Science and Engineering Fair. Some students preparing projects for these fairs may qualify to enter their work in other science competitions as well.

While there are numerous alternative science programs and competitions, this section covers the four largest: the Intel Science Talent Search, the Siemens Competition, the National Junior Science and Humanities Symposium, and the Discovery Channel Young Scientist Challenge.

Intel Science Talent Search

This is considered one of the oldest and most prestigious science competitions in the United States. Like the Intel International Science and Engineering Fair and the Discovery Channel Young Scientist Challenge, this competition is administered through Science Service. Several past alumni of the Science Talent Search have become Nobel laureates in physics and chemistry, recipients of the Fields Medal in Mathematics, the National Medal of Science, and many other prestigious awards and distinctions.

From nearly 2,000 completed entry forms and application materials received every year, 300 semifinalists are initially selected who, along with their schools, receive a matching cash award. Then, from this group of 300 semifinalists, 40 finalists are selected to attend the National Academy of Sciences for the Science Talent Institute in Washington, D.C. to exhibit their research and compete for the grand prize of a four-year $100,000 scholarship. In addition to the grand prize there are substantial scholarships for students in second through tenth place, and the remaining 30 finalists are guaranteed a minimum scholarship of $5,000. First-through tenth-place scholarships are disbursed in eight equal installments to the college at which the winning students matriculate. The 30 finalists receiving the $5,000 scholarships receive their award money upon graduation from high school.

In order to participate in this program, students must be in their last year of high school and have completed their college entrance requirements by October

1 of their senior year. The research project submitted must be the work of a single student (team projects are not eligible). The student's report must not exceed 20 pages along with the research report. The student and his or her teacher or adviser must submit completed entry forms along with the student's official high school transcripts, class rank, and standardized test scores. While every aspect of a student's entry form factors into his or her chances of winning the competition, the research report is given the most weight by the judging panel of prestigious scientists, mathematicians, and engineers. The deadline for submission of all materials is in mid-November of each year.

For more information on this contest or how to obtain forms for participation, contact Science Service, 1719 N Street, N.W., Washington, D.C. 20036. Telephone (202) 785-2255 or visit them online at www.sciserv.org/sts.

Discovery Channel Young Scientist Challenge

The Discovery Channel Young Scientist Challenge (DCYSC) for students in grades 5-8 began in 1999. This competition is administered by Science Service and funded by Discovery Communications, Inc. The top 10 percent of students winning at a state or regional DCYSC affiliated fair are eligible for nomination in the DCYSC. These nominees win various awards and receive an entry booklet for the national competition. Students are required to submit their entries by a June deadline in order to compete to become one of 400 semifinalists. Forty finalists win an all-expense-paid trip to Washington, D.C., to compete for a variety of scholarships, prizes, and internships in the month of October.

For more information on this contest or how to obtain forms for participation, contact Science Service, 1719 N Street, N.W., Washington, D.C. 20036. Telephone (202) 785-2255 or visit them online at www.sciserv.org/dysc.

Siemens Westinghouse Competition

This competition is funded by the Siemens Foundation and is administered by the College Board and Educational Testing Service (the same group that created the SAT). It draws about 1,200 high school contestants annually comprising both individual and team projects. Entries are evaluated purely on scientific merit. Winners from various regional competitions advance to the national level where individual contestants compete for a top prize of a $100,000 scholarship and team projects compete for a top team prize of $100,000 that is split among the team members. In addition to the top scholarship prizes are a number of other significant scholarship prizes for students in second through sixth place as well as smaller cash prizes for regional finalists and winners.

The deadline for submission of application materials is October 1 of every year.

For more information on this contest or how to obtain forms for participation, contact the Siemens Foundation, 170 Wood Ave. South, Iselin, NJ 08830. Telephone (877) 822-5233 or visit them online at www.siemens-foundation.org.

Junior Science and Humanities Symposium

The Junior Science and Humanities Symposium has been sponsored by the U.S. Army since 1958 and was joined in sponsorship by the U.S. Navy and U.S. Air Force in 1995. This competition is open to students in grades 9–12 who have completed a significant research project in science, engineering, or mathematics. Nearly 10,000 students compete annually from the United States and its territories as well as Department of Defense schools in Europe and the Pacific rim. Judging initially occurs at 48 different regional symposiums. To qualify for a regional competition, students must be nominated by their school. Selected students then present their research at the regional level before a panel of judges. The top five winners from each regional competition earn the honor to compete at the National Junior Science and Humanities Symposium for scholarships of various amounts. The top eight national winners also receive an all-expenses-paid trip to the London International Youth Science Forum.

Most regional symposiums have deadlines for school nominations in early December. For more information on this contest or how to obtain forms for participation, contact Junior Science and Humanities Symposium, 24 Warren St., Concord, NH 03301. Telephone (603) 228-4520 or visit them online at www.jshs.org.

GLOSSARY

abstract A brief summary of a science project (approx. 300 words) that explains the project's objective and procedure and provides generalized data and a workable solution to the problem addressed by the project.

backboard A self-supporting bulletin board with a summary outline of a science project. The backboard contains the project title and topic progression, together with flowcharts, photographs, and other significant project descriptions. The backboard is usually organized according to the steps of the scientific method.

biological sciences category A basic category encompassing several life sciences, including behavioral and social sciences, biochemistry, botany, ecology, genetics, medicine and health, microbiology, zoology, animal species studies, disease, etc.

clarity A judging criterion that addresses whether a science project is presented in a concise fashion.

conclusion The solution to a proposed issue and confirmation or rejection of a hypothesis.

control A part of an experiment that provides a guideline for comparing an experimental group.

creative ability A judging criterion that grades ingenuity and originality in an approach to a topic.

data Recorded information that is organized for final analysis and observation.

dependent variable The variable that is being measured.

Discovery Channel Young Scientist Challenge (DCYSC) Since 1999 this science fair, administered by Science Service, has been held for the top science fair projects for students in grades 5–8.

display The complete set-up of a science project. The display includes a backboard, a representation of the subject matter or experimental results, and a research report.

dramatic value A judging criterion that addresses whether the project is presented in a way that attracts attention through the use of graphics and layout.

erroneous hypothesis An incorrect or vague hypothesis that does not support the experimental results.

experiment The part of the project in which the scientist tests to verify a law, explain a cause-and-effect relationship, measure efficiency, or observe an unexplained process.

experimental angle The narrowed experimental option best suited to bringing about a desired or fitting solution to the issue.

flow chart A diagram that describes the results of a process, steps or sequence through the use of various geometric shapes from beginning to end.

frequency distribution   A mathematical summary of a set of data that shows the numerical frequency of each class of items.

histogram   A graph that represents a frequency distribution. The item classes are placed along the horizontal axis and the frequencies along the vertical axis. Rectangles are drawn, with the item class as the base and the frequency as the side.

hypothesis   An assumed or tentative guess as to the possible solution to a problem.

independent variable   The variable that is controlled or manipulated by the experimenter.

Intel International Science and Engineering Fair (Intel ISEF)   Since 1949, this science fair administered by Science Service has been held for the top science fair projects from around the world. It is considered to be the "Super Bowl" of science fairs.

journal   A logbook used to record everything that the student has learned and completed with his or her project. Items to note include articles read, places visited, data results, etc.

line graph   A graph used to summarize information from a table. It has an x (horizontal) axis and a y (vertical) axis, where points are plotted at corresponding regions.

mean   The measurement of the central location of a group of data through the use of a mathematical average. The mean is denoted by the symbol $(\bar{x})$.

percentile   The position of one value from a set of data that expresses the percentage of the other data that lie below this value. The position of a particular percentile can be calculated by dividing the desired percentile by 100 and multiplying by the number of items in the ascending data set.

physical sciences category   A basic category including chemistry, math, earth and space science, engineering, physics, toxic waste, electronics, etc.

pie chart   A graph represented by a circle that is divided into segments. The circle represents the whole amount (100%), and each section represents a percentage of the whole.

primary sources   Those sources of information that consist of surveys, observations, and experiments done directly by the science student.

procedural plan   A uniform and systematic way of testing the subject matter. Procedural planning begins with correlating to determine variables and a uniform control group.

project display   The item(s) from a science project that can fully represent, exemplify, or explain research, experimentation, and conclusions.

project limitation guidelines   Guidelines established by the ISEF that explain how far a student may go in his or her research and experimentation.

purpose/objective   The goal of a project; the theme that requires greater development or understanding.

qualitative analysis   A means of analysis that is based on the findings in an experiment.

quantitative analysis   A means of analysis that is based on measurements in an experiment (always involves numbers).

research   The process by which information about the issue at hand is collected to search for possible clues in the development of the purpose or objective.

research report   An in-depth discussion of an entire science project from start to finish, including a subject history, research experience, method applied, experimental angle used, data, conclusive remarks, glossary, photos, diagrams, etc.

science fair An exhibition of selectively chosen science projects grouped into corresponding categories and marked for their quality. Science fairs occur on local, state, regional, and international levels. (The fairs discussed in this book refer to those affiliated with the International Science and Engineering Fair.)

science project A project of a scientific nature that is done by students in grades 6–12 for a local, state, regional, or international science exhibition. The project employs a systematic approach in order to formulate a conclusion to a proposed scientific question. The science project is modeled after the scientific method.

scientific abstracts Bound volumes of thousands of brief scientific discussions. Scientific abstracts are grouped into two classes: research and experimental. The abstracts discuss experimental reports and review scientific literature.

scientific approach A judging criterion that addresses how a science project shows evidence of an applied scientific or engineering development through cause-and-effect, verification of laws, applied techniques for efficiency, or presentation of a new concept.

scientific method An organized process used to form the basis of a science fair project consisting of a problem/purpose, hypothesis, research/procedure, experiment, and conclusion.

scientific review committee (SRC) A group of science fair officials that enforces various rules and criteria for conducting and completing a science fair project.

secondary sources Sources of information written by outsiders and obtained through libraries, media, government agencies, or corporations.

skill A judging criterion that grades a science project on how much scientific and engineering practice was employed. The level of experimentation, preparation, and treatment of the subject matter play an important role.

statistical method A method used to further describe and summarize data results through the use of specialized numbers, graphs, and charts.

table An orderly display of data, usually arranged in rows and columns.

tests and surveys The techniques that endeavor to determine the relationship, if any, that exists between variables.

timeline A diagram that shows various results or measurements that have been recorded at various stages at specific times.

thoroughness A judging criterion that addresses the variety and depth of the literature used, experimental investigation, and all the aspects of the project.

variable Some characteristic of an object, environment, plant, animal, performance, or behavior that can take on two or more values.

INDEX

abstracts, scientific, 16, 46, 49
acid rain and *Spirogyra,* 118–20
accuracy, 51
airborne pollution, 114–15
airfoil lift and angles of attack, 170–71
alcohol as a fuel, 99–101
alcohol dependency in rat, 127–29
algae
 Eremosphaera, 73–75
 Spirogyra, 118–20
algae cells, effect of electro-magnetic fields on, 73–75
analysis, 33, 34, 35–40, 41
antibacterial effects of garlic, 160–63
antibiotics, dandelions as, 138–140
aquatic life and heavy metals, 121–24
awards, 5, 7, 54–55, 221, 222, 223
axes, 36–37, 39

Bach's music, mathematical patterns in, 92–93
backboards, 42–44, 45, 49
bacteria. *See* microbiology
bar graphs, 41
bees, attracting, 59–61
behavioral science, 50
 attracting bees, 59–61
 gender identity and short-term memory, 62–64
Bernoulli's principle, 87, 88
biochemistry, 50
biodegradability of plastic, paper, and newspaper, 116–18
biological sciences, 50, 55
botany, 50
 cancer in plants, 70–72
 cloning of plants, 68–69
 electromagnetic fields and algae cells, 73–75
 plant transpiration rate, 65–67

cancer in plants, 70–72
cheating in baseball, 181–184
chemistry
 dyes in drink mixes and marking pens, 89–91

filtration abilities of lobster shell chitin, 80–82
 melting ice, 76–77
 pH and corrosion of iron and copper, 78–79
 saltwater mixing in estuaries, 83–85
 soap bubble life span, 86–88
clam safety, 150–51
clarity, 51–52
cloning of plants, 68–69
colorblindness in dogs, 192–94
computer science/mathematics, 50, 92–93
conclusions, 10, 32, 35, 41, 42
control groups, 31–32, 33, 34
copper, corrosion of, 78–79
correlations, 39
creative ability, 51
criteria, 51, 43, 55
cubical earth effects, 178–80
Curtin, Brian, 151

D'Amato, Nicole, 123
dandelions as antibiotics, 138–140
data, 32–36, 38–41, 54
deadlines, 27
dependent variables, 30–31
Discovery Channel Young Scientist Challenge, 6, 7
displays, 42–49
distillation, 100
dramatic value, 52
dyes in drink mixes and marking pens, 89–91

earth science, 50
earthworm recycling system, 102–106
electromagnetic fields and algae cells, 73–75
energy
 alcohol as a fuel, 99–101
 brightness of incandescent light bulb, 94–96
 insulation effectiveness, 97–98
engineering, 26, 50, 51
environmental science, 50
 acid rain and *Spirogyra,* 118–20

airborne particle pollution, 114–15
 biodegradability of plastic, paper, and newspaper, 116–18
 earthworm recycling system, 102–106
 heavy metals and aquatic life, 121–24
 lawn and pristine water, 105–106
 oil spill effects, 110–111
 soil around gas stations, 107–109
equipment, 21, 32, 58
Eremosphaera algae, 73–75
exhibits, 42. *See also* displays
experimental groups, 31–34
experimental procedural plans, 30–32, 34
experiments, 26–28, 30–33, 34

fermentation, 100
filtration abilities of lobster shell chitin, 80–82
flow charts, 40, 41
footwear vs. bacteria, 152–53
forms, required, 21, 22, 28–29
fuel, alcohol as a, 99–101

garlic as antibacterial, 160–63
gender identity and short-term memory, 62–64
golf ball's bounce and distance, 185–87
graphing data, 35, 36–40, 41

health science
 alcohol dependency in rat, 127–29
 tooth cleaners, 125–26
 ultraviolet radiation protection, 130–32
heavy metals and aquatic life, 121–24
histogram, 39
hypotheses, 9, 30, 32, 33, 34

ice, melting, 76–77
incandescent bulb, brightness of, 94–96
independent variables, 30–31
Institutional Review Board, 22

insulation effectiveness, 97–98
Intel International Science and Engineering Fair, 6–8, 11, 18, 21, 22, 28, 47, 49
Intel Science Talent Search, 46
Internet, 16, 21
interviews, 53–54
iron, corrosion of, 78–79

journals, 16, 20, 26, 35
judging, 26, 27, 33, 51
Junior Science and Humanities Symposium, 46

Karanian, David, 129

lawn and pristine water, 105–106
letters, to resource people, 22, 23, 24
light bulb, brightness of, 94–96
lobster shell chitin as filter, 80–82

magazines, 16
mathematics, 50
    mathematical patterns in Bach's music, 92–93
    the wave and golden mean, 133–37
mean, 38
measurements, 33, 35
medicine and health, 50
memory, gender identity and short-term, 62–64
mentors, 20, 23–25, 32
microbiology, 50
    bacteria and heavy metals in sewage, 148–49
    bacteria in waterbeds, 143–45
    clam safety, 150–51
    dandelions as antibiotics, 138–140
    food molds to reduce rabbit bacteria, 141–42
    footwear vs. bacteria, 152–5
    garlic as antibacterial, 160–63
    p-traps, 154–56, 157–59
molds to reduce rabbit bacteria, 141–42

networking, 42
newspapers, 24

objectives, defining, 27, 34
oil spill effects, 110–111
origami wave and golden mean, 133–37
Orzel, Katherine, 155

pendulum's period of motion, 164–66

percentile, 39–40
periodicals, 16
Peterson, Celeste, 191
pH and corrosion of iron and copper, 78–79
physical sciences, 50, 55
physics, 50
    airfoil lift and angles of attack, 170–71
    cheating in baseball, 181–184
    chicken embryo heartbeat, 190–92
    colorblindness in dogs, 192–94
    cubical earth effects, 178–80
    golf ball's bounce and distance, 185–87
    pendulum's period of motion, 164–66
    polarization and stress in airplane windows, 172–74
    relaxing new pet fish, 188–189
    shape and viscous effect, 175–77
    solid wood vs. composites, 167–69
pie charts, 37–38, 40, 41
plants. See botany
plotting, of graphs, 36
polarization and stress in airplane windows, 172–74
poster sessions, 42, 43
problem, in scientific method, 9, 28
procedural errors, 32–33, 34
procedures, 10
proposals, project, 20
p-traps, 154–56, 157–59
qualitative analysis, 35
quantitative analysis, 35
questions, 9, 26–28

rabbit bacteria, food molds to reduce, 141–42
relaxing new pet fish, 188–189
reports, 44–46, 49
research, 9, 20, 26, 29–30
results, 10, 26, 27, 32–35, 39–41

saltwater mixing in estuaries, 83–85
science fair projects
    alternative competitions, 21, 23
    awards for, 5, 7
    categories of, 22–25, 50, 55
    contacts for, 22–25
    individuals or teams, 11, 12
    judging of, 26, 27, 33, 51
    organizing and planning, 20–22, 26–32, 26–28

mentors for, 23–25
rules for, 21–22, 28–29, 49
scientific method in, 9–10, 12, 26
selecting topic for, 13–20, 25, 27–28
setting up, 50–51
Science Fair Supply, 43
science fairs
    benefits of participating in, 5, 7
    list of, 216–20
    local, 6
    state and regional, 6, 18, 19, 51, 55
    workshops, 18
Science Service, Inc., 6, 7
scientific method, 9–10, 12, 26, 35
Scientific Review Committee, 20, 21–22, 28, 46, 47
scientific supply companies, 21, 32, 58, 208–210
sewage, bacteria and heavy metal in, 148–49
shape and viscous effect, 175–77
Showboard, 43
soap bubble life span, 86–88
soil around gas stations, 107–109
sources of information, 45
space science, 50
Spirogyra algae, 118–20
statistical method, 38–40, 41
supplies, 21, 32, 58, 208–210

tabulating data, 35–46, 41
testing hypotheses, 29
thoroughness, 51
time line, 40
tooth cleaners, 125–26
topics, selecting, 13–20, 25, 27–28
transpiration rate of plants, 65–67
trials, repeated, 32, 33, 34

ultraviolet radiation protection, 130–32
unexpected results, 33

variables, 30

waterbeds, bacteria in, 143–45
Web sites, 16, 29
wood composites vs. solid wood, 167–69
workshops, 18–19

zoology, 50